Photograph of Rashid Halloway. *Photo courtesy of Bud Smith Photography Inc.*

Chapter 1-6 and Conclusions

Rashid A. Halloway

The following chapters and conclusions represent the words of Rashid A. Halloway in his unpublished manuscript discovered after his death. The text of the chapters and conclusion have been kept as close to the original words of Professor Halloway as possible, save minor corrections in punctuation and formatting as needed. The notes and references have been updated to reflect the format of the publisher.

Germany, Poland, and the Danzig Question, 1937–1939

Germany, Poland, and the Danzig Question, 1937–1939

Rashid A. Halloway
Introduction by John Shosky
Preface by Elfa Halloway

HAMILTON BOOKS
AN IMPRINT OF
ROWMAN & LITTLEFIELD
Lanham • Boulder • New York • London

Published by Hamilton Books
An imprint of The Rowman & Littlefield Publishing Group, Inc.
4501 Forbes Boulevard, Suite 200, Lanham, Maryland 20706
www.rowman.com

6 Tinworth Street, London SE11 5AL, United Kingdom

Copyright © 2021 by The Rowman & Littlefield Publishing Group, Inc.

All rights reserved. No part of this book may be reproduced in any form or by any electronic or mechanical means, including information storage and retrieval systems, without written permission from the publisher, except by a reviewer who may quote passages in a review.

British Library Cataloguing in Publication Information Available

Library of Congress Cataloging-in-Publication Data Available

Library of Congress Control Number: 2021931237
ISBN 978-0-7618-7227-6 (pbk) |
ISBN 978-0-7618-7228-3 (ebook)

To the author's Mother, Yema Caulker
His Father Abdul-Hussein
His Son Hillel
And to the men and women of Africa who battle on in the face of great odds.

Contents

Acknowledgments	xi
Preface by Elfa Halloway	xiii
Introduction by John Shosky	xv
1 Setting the Stage	1
2 The Teschen Problem, September–October 1938	13
3 The Stage Is Set	23
4 The Polish Ultimatum to the Danzig Senate	39
5 The Tug-of-War for the Soviet Alliance	47
6 The Failure of the British Mediation	59
Conclusions	65
Bibliography	73
Index	79
About the Author and Contributors	83

Acknowledgments

What guided me, to quote Winston Churchill, was "Never give in, never, never, never." (Winston Churchill, October 29, 1941. National Churchill Museum, Winston Churchill, Speeches, 1941–1946 Speeches). And so, above all I thank my Maker for keeping me and pushing me again and again to undertake the many unfamiliar steps and tasks necessary to prepare this manuscript for publication. Many have helped and guided me along this arduous path covering many years—Patti Belcher, Brooke Bascietto, Victoria Koulakjian, and Brooke Bures, Associate Editor, Rowman & Littlefield; copy editor Christy Parrish first; then Sam Brawand whose expertise, together with Brooke Bures, brought the manuscript to fruition. When I was out of my depth on Russian, Janet Spikes at the Wilson Center Library came to the rescue, and my good friend Dr. Mika Popovic laid to rest my last doubts. A friend from my German Embassy days in London, Ruediger von Pachelbel, Amb. ret'd. provided background of the era. I dug into Rashid's past and brazenly called people I had only heard about—Dr. Eva Wagner, Linacre House, Oxford University (1962), Monica Popa and Marsaleete Anderson, Alumni Relations Officers and later Dr. Anne Keene, Director of the Development Office, Linacre College, ret'd. A special thank you is reserved for Paul Slack, retired principal of Linacre and David Brown, his successor, for their encouragement and facilitation.

I am indebted to Professor Emerita Anna M. Cienciala of the Department of History, University of Kansas, for her comprehensive commenting, Rashid's friend, Prof. Dr. Robert Johnston, formerly of Georgia State University who thoroughly reviewed the manuscript and told me that his conclusion of events differed somewhat from the author's! I thank Dr. Hamid Taqi, Rashid's childhood friend and colleague at Morehouse College, for corroborating information, telling me that Rashid had curiosity, wisdom, and far-reaching interests in the political sciences.

I am deeply indebted to Linacre alumnus Prof. John Shosky for his comprehensive Introduction.

Gregory Griffiths, Rashid's student at Morehouse and now a judge in Montgomery, Alabama, reconnected me with Morehouse faculty, notably Prof. Abraham Davis, Ph.D. (ret'd).

I thank the many who supported this project over the years and who will be pleased that it is completed—last but not least, our son Hillel and Monica Welham for their research, Hiam Halawi for her translation from the French, our families—the Halloways, the Halawis, the Oldenburgs, and the Danapels, and my sister Karin Schlegel.

EH

Preface

Between submitting this manuscript to University Press of America (UPA) and receiving acceptance, death occurred—death of the author Rashid A. Halloway. The story is more involved—UPA sent the letter of acceptance to Linacre College, University of Oxford where the author—my husband—spent the summer of 1979 working on his doctoral thesis. In late July, Rashid returned to the United States a dying man. Peter Holloway, bursar at Linacre, rerouted the package to me in Maryland. This was in October of 1979; Rashid had died in mid-August. I had been unaware of the submission. It was so sad; it was all too late. Or, could I do it?

While UPA was still willing to publish, I was too busy with work and raising our son Hillel. It was not until 2007 that I called them. The manuscript underwent a fresh review (the old file was long gone) and to my great joy, Rashid's work was again accepted.

In a blink of an eye, ten years had gone by, and still no book.

Now Rowman & Littlefield Publishing Group, the UPA honors the 2007 agreement. We persevered in getting this little book published to honor Rashid's many gifts: his great understanding, his clear thinking, his eloquent speaking and elegant writing—and last but not least—his warm laughter, his expert cooking, and entertaining dancing! Rashid was at home at a party, at a lectern, and the negotiating table during his tenure as Trade Attaché at the Sierra Leone High Commission, London.

Rashid Halloway was, to use a metaphor, one of the best diamonds Sierra Leone has produced. His friends—and his foes—knew that. The obstacles put in his way were many. His one ambition, to be given the opportunity of restructuring the Sierra Leone Foreign Service, was scuttled by politics. Naiñ dat!

Thank you, UPA and Rowman & Littlefield, for enabling us to finish what Rashid began so long ago.

Elfa Halloway
November 2020

Introduction
Rashid Halloway: Scholar, Diplomat, Teacher

John Shosky

This brief book is great work of scholarship.[1] It is about the German desire for Danzig as a catalyst for the Second World War, a view now substantially documented by many other scholars. The redrawing of Europe after the First World War gave Danzig independent status as a free state.[2] However, German leaders cast envious eyes on the port city. Poland felt that the city was historically and culturally Polish. Historical and cultural claims remained a heated topic of conversation in both Germany and Poland. Starting in 1938, German demands for the return of Danzig substantially increased tensions in Europe.[3] The Polish Foreign Minister, Józef Beck, called it a "war of nerves." On January 5, 1939, German Chancellor Adolph Hitler told Beck that Danzig must become German. That view was reiterated again on March 20th by German Foreign Minister Joachim von Ribbentrop. Danzig may not have been a tipping point, but a German Danzig was a condition for peace and a cause for war. Amid the swirling events of 1939, the status of Danzig was an important variable in the discussion of German policy and planning, along with the disposition of Austria, the Sudetenland, and later the invasion of Poland. On September 1, 1939, at 4:45 a.m., the German training ship Schleswig Holstein opened fire on the Polish fort of Westerplatte, near Danzig. The Second World War had begun. Danzig was occupied by the German army. Hitler gleefully went to see his conquest. Its strategic importance was obvious, with access to the Baltic Sea and beyond. However, Danzig's role in the conflict has been generally forgotten, marginalized, becoming just a talking point among most scholars. Halloway wanted to demonstrate its centrality in the conflict. And, his view has been vindicated by the scholarship of later historians. And now this book takes its rightful place alongside the outstanding historical efforts of Norman Davies, Richard Overy, and others.[4]

This book also has an interesting publication history. It has been a piece of buried treasure, now newly unearthed and restored. It comes back to us after a disappearance of three decades. Originally accepted for publication by the University Press of America (UPA) before the death of Rashid Halloway in 1979, *Germany, Poland and the Danzig Question* remained stratified in his papers until uncovered and resubmitted in 2007. The UPA deserves much credit for making this vital piece of scholarship available after all these years, fulfilling its commitment to a gifted teacher and a brilliant student of Africa and the world. His wife, Elfa, has shown steadfast and loving commitment in recovering the manuscript and finding a way to honor Halloway's intention to publish.

Rashid A. Halloway was born on September 12, 1936 in Gandama, Sierra Leone. He grew up in the days of simmering unrest with the British administration and Empire, the days when colonialism chaffed and scarred, but unrest was rare and independence seemed like a dream. Like many of the talented boys his own age, he looked to education as the way out, just as African Americans used education as a road to freedom in the 1950s and 1960s in the United States. He became a student of great promise, attending the Albert Academy Secondary School, Freetown, Sierra Leone, and graduating in 1952. Like many students of ability, he knew that future opportunities were dependent on leaving Africa for an education abroad. So he applied to Ohio State University in the United States, where he was accepted in 1955, earning a Bachelor of Arts degree in International Relations in 1959. While in the United States, he became politically active. He was elected a senator in the university's student government and National President of the All-Africa Students Union of the United States and Canada. As a keen sportsman, he represented the university in soccer and was a keen tennis player. As a speaker, he was elected a member of the National Forensic League of the United States. Upon graduation, he attended the London School of Economics and Political Science (LSE), where he trained in preparation for the Sierra Leone Foreign Service. In fact, he was appointed to the Foreign Service as an administrative cadet assistant. However, he refused the appointment to attend the University of Oxford and read for a D.Phil.

Fortunately, he arrived in 1962 at the moment when Oxford was increasing its commitment to graduate students. Halloway was admitted to the first class of students at Linacre House, named for the classical scholar, humanist, and physician Thomas Linacre (c. 1460-1524).[5] In the 1950s, the University was confronted with a growing number of graduate students. One solution under discussion was to create a new college, followed by two additional graduate colleges. Starting in 1956, plans for a graduate college began to emerge as part of the transition of St. Catherine's Society, founded in 1868 and housing undergraduate and graduate students, into an undergraduate college. The graduate students would find a home in a new community, which eventually became Linacre College.[6] As part of the plan, Linacre House as it was known then, was set up as a Department of the University with a Principal, Senior Members, and a small administrative staff. In October 1962, Linacre House opened its doors for 135 graduates in residence (some went to other colleges—the initial Linacre entry class had eighty students). The international flavor of resident students in the college was noticeable. There were thirty-five different nationalities: fifty-two students were from Europe (including the United Kingdom), twenty-nine from North America, sixteen from Asia and the Far East, seven from the Middle East, and six from Latin America and the Caribbean (Some students did not fit into these categories).[7] Halloway was one of those students, attending on a Commonwealth Scholarship. He had come a long way from Gandama.

The principal was John Bamborough ("Bam"), a well-known scholar who was a perfect fit for the new college: personable, scholarly, and visionary. The junior members could come from all disciplines. The senior members were originally drawn from university lecturers who were not at that time Fellows of traditional colleges. There was only one common room, shared by senior and junior members. In 1965, the status of Linacre changed: it became a college. As a small graduate college, with constant interaction between students and fellows, it developed its own personality and culture, becoming an intimate, warm academic environment—a culture that persists to this day. Recollections of that time are filled with pleasant memories of the welcome given to graduates, their families or partners, and children. Scholarship met the highest standards, but in a more relaxed atmosphere. As Professor Rom Harré recalled in his eulogy of Bamborough in 2009, "Bam realized from the beginning that Linacre would not prosper unless it provided an alternative centre of gravity to the departments and faculty centres where most of the members of the College, junior and senior, spent their days."[8]

So one of the distinguishing characteristics of the college was its family atmosphere. It helped separate the college from its sister institutions. This approach drew occasional scornful comments from some of the older dons in the ancient colleges. But it made Linacre students closer, with a stronger bond to the college . . . a community that did not end with graduation but ripened into life-long friendships and a high rate of college marriages.

Halloway was the Common Room president, responsible for a number of social and intellectual activities, as well as representing the graduate students in the Governing Body meetings. He was the first African ever elected as Common Room President in either Oxford or the University of Cambridge. Colin Newbury, in his history of Linacre College, called Halloway an "extrovert and entertaining."[9] The first librarian, Eva Wagner, calls him "daemonic . . . whose 'Blueprints for Peace' were terrifying."[10] Elfa Halloway says he was "handsome, thoughtful, the center of attention, fun."[11] Halloway was a congenial and constant presence in the College, mentioned in the college minutes for his organization, social skills, and willingness to buy drinks. In fact, his late payment of his Common Room fees was a persistent concern (eventually settled, as Newbury notes, by the Sierra Leone High Commissioner's Office). "Rashid was a very popular fellow, remembers Professor Harré. "He was always the life of the party. In fact, he gave the best parties. The wine was always excellent, a step above the normal. The food was good. His parties were not to be missed. When he went to a party he was always good company, laughing and smiling and very talkative."[12]

In keeping with collegiate tradition, a discussion society was set up in the college named after Thomas Bradwardine (c. 1290–1349), an early Oxford polymath. However, Rashid found it too philosophical for his taste and founded the Hammarskjold Society (named after the late Secretary General of the United Nations) as a forum for political discussions. Both societies flourished and eventually merged to become the Hammerdine Society.

Halloway was particularly close to now Principal Bamborough, who attended his wedding to Elfa. The word "Bam" means "older brother" in Sierra Leone, and Bamborough functioned as an older brother and mentor to Rashid during his time in college.

Events overtook Halloway at Oxford. In 1963, he became a part-time diplomat in the Sierra Leone High Commission. Part of his work was to act as a liaison for the Commonwealth Finance Ministers' Consultative Conference and for the Commonwealth Prime Ministers' Conference. Then, in 1965, he was appointed Commercial Attaché, a post he held for three years until a military take-over deposed the Sierra Leone government. During those three years he led delegations around the world, with a memorable leadership role in signing the Final Act of the Kennedy Round of the *General Agreement on Tariffs and Trade* (*GATT*) in Geneva. His diplomatic duties eventually took him away from Linacre and Oxford. He was never able to finish his degree, although amazingly he did fulfill the course and residency requirements, as well as write a thesis, "A Study of the Afro-Asian States in the United Nations Organization from 1950-1962." However, his thesis was never submitted. In an undated letter, clearly from this time, he said that he hoped after Oxford to either return as a scholar at the University of Sierra Leone or to enter the diplomatic service of his country. If he became a lecturer, he hoped to teach African politics in emerging states or theories in international relations. He also mentions that he has been at work on a manuscript on German-Polish relations between the years 1938-1939, clearly the genesis of the present book.

In 1970, he found himself across the Atlantic in Washington, DC, as executive director of the African Heritage Foundation. Later, he also became the director of the International African Chamber of Commerce.

In 1971, he accepted a university teaching position . . . not in his native country but in Atlanta, at the prestigious Morehouse College, the "Black Harvard." He held this position until his death in 1979. It was an exciting time, an energetic moment, with Morehouse on the cutting-edge of liberal thinking, and an inspiring training ground for the civil rights movement. The college had benefitted greatly from the twenty-seven-year presidency of Dr. Benjamin Elijah Mays, a powerful figure in the civil rights movement and mentor to Dr. Martin Luther King, Jr., future Atlanta mayor Maynard Jackson, future President George H. W. Bush's cabinet member Louis W. Sullivan, and many of the great "Morehouse Men."[13] When Halloway arrived, the school's new president was Hugh Gloster, a former diplomat and a committed voice for international education. Halloway was hired as an assistant professor of political science and soon was appointed the director of a new program in international studies. He was urged to use his connections to bring international figures, especially from developing nations, to Morehouse. In one year Halloway brought in, among others, the Pakistani Ambassador to the People's Republic of China, Agha Shahi; the World Bank's Paul Danquah from Ghana; Dr. John Karefa-Smart, who at that time was on the faculty at Harvard University and a well-known political figure from Sierra Leone (later a presidential candidate there); Nigerian novelist Mkem Nwanko; and Dr. Shyamali Harris, an Indian physician who specialized in breast cancer.

He was a well-regarded teacher. Pictures from that time period show Halloway as energetic, passionate, and serious. Elfa remembers Halloway talking about the people who influenced his life and work, people like "Winston Churchill, Dean Acheson, Dag Hammarskjöld, Ralph Bunche, Dr. Martin Luther King, Jr., Senator Hubert H. Humphrey, the philosopher Ludwig Wittgenstein, and Dr. Mays." He also spoke of African leaders whom he admired, like "Kwame Nkrumah, Patrice Lumumba, Jomo Kenyatta, and Nelson Mandela." And he spoke of Dr. Karefa-Smart, who had a distinguished career at the World Health Organization and in United National People's Party in Sierra Leone. Halloway gave numerous speeches on civil rights and was actively in opposition to colonialism in Africa. Elfa remembers that he drew attention from the authorities in the United States and had a "thick file" at immigration.[14]

His premature death in 1979 was a tragedy, a voice silenced too soon. In this book that voice regains an audience. And Halloway left a number of papers and unpublished manuscripts. In one of them, titled "Beyond Civilization," Halloway speculates about our purpose in life. He writes

> Hardship, breakdown and crisis are excellent, if somewhat harsh, teachers. To live with catastrophe, our lot today, we must come to terms with it. Then, maybe, we would discover its hidden purpose too – to make us change, seek for new foundations. The crisis of civilization, on everybody's lips now, perhaps points beyond civilization.... It is not distorting history to say that, coming from entirely different backgrounds, yet united in aim and effort, there is in our midst a growing, invisible brotherhood, a fellowship of the future. Man grows when inspired by a high vision. Can there be anything more dangerous, beautiful and necessary than the remaking of modern man and society? It is our date with destiny, to be civilized beyond civilization.[15]

In this book he reminds us of the thin crust of civilization, when nationalism and war, envy and conquest, tested the civilizing commitment of Europe. When the horrors of war were inflicted on the world, it was saved by those who met their "date with destiny," with powerful and bloody consequences, hoping that force would ultimately lead to a new era "civilized beyond civilization."

John Shosky
Visiting Senior Member
Linacre College
University of Oxford
November 2010

NOTES

1. Thanks to Elfa Halloway, Anne Keene and Rom Harré for reviewing a draft of this introduction. Also, many thanks to Elfa for allowing access to Rashid's unpublished papers.

2. Margaret MacMillan, *Paris 1919: Six Months that Changed the World* (New York: Random House, 2003).

3. Jerzy Lukowski and Hubert Zawadzki, *A Concise History of Poland* (Cambridge: Cambridge University Press, 2001).

4. See Norman Davies, *Rising '44: The Battle for Warsaw* (New York: Viking, 2003); Richard Overy, *1939: Countdown to War* (New York: Viking Press, 2009).

5. *Essays on the Life and Work of Thomas Linacre, c. 1460-1524*, ed. Francis Maddison, Margaret Pelling, and Charles Webster (Oxford: Clarendon Press, 1977).

6. See Colin Newbury, "The Origins of Linacre College, 1956-1965," *Linacre Journal* 1 (June 1997): 5-27; and G. R. Evans, *The University of Oxford: A New History* (London: I. B. Tauris, 2010).

7. See Morehouse College, *Morehouse College Bulletin* (Winter 1972): 8-9; and (Spring 1973): 20-21.

8. Rom Harré, "Memorial Service, 20th June 2009 University Church of St Mary the Virgin, A Tribute," in *Linacre News, John Bernard Bamborough 1921-2009, Memorial Publication* (Oxford: Linacre College, 2009), 6-7.

9. Newbury, "The Origins of Linacre College," 6-7.

10. Eva Wagner, "Nostalgia," *Linacre Lines* (Michaelmas 2006): 12, http://www.linacre.ox.ac.uk/sites/default/files/michaelmas_2006.pdf (accessed January 14, 2018).

11. Elfa Halloway, Personal conversation with John Shosky, Washington, DC, October 2010.

12. Rom Harré, Personal conversation with John Shosky, Oxford, November 2010.

13. Benjamin E. Mays, *Born to Rebel: An Autobiography*. (New York: Scribner, 1971; repr. Athens: University of Georgia Press, 1987).

14. Elfa Halloway, Personal conversation with John Shosky, Washington, DC, October 2010.

15. Rashid A. Halloway, "Beyond Civilization," unpublished manuscript.

Chapter 1

Setting the Stage: Polish Efforts to Issue a Joint German-Polish Declaration on Danzig

The Treaty of Versailles did not, in the German view, settle the nationalities problem in Eastern Europe.[1] The Post-World War I Governments in Germany never accepted as final the Western frontier of Poland and hoped for a day when arrangements on territorial disputes would be reached with Poland. In this context the German-Polish Non-Aggression Treaty of January 26, 1934, was also regarded as provisional by the Germans.[2] Both Governments declared that it was "their intention to reach direct understanding on problems concerning their mutual relations" and in "no case, however, shall they have recourse to force in order to settle such questions under dispute." The Treaty did not exclude that "the guarantee of peace established upon the above principles will facilitate for both Governments the important task of finding, for political, economic, and cultural problems, solutions based upon just and equitable considerations of the interests of both countries."[3]

The Government in Warsaw was aware of the fact that the 1934 Treaty was not a final peace pact ("Friedensgarantie"). Piłsudski did not think that peace would last for the next ten years. In the Marshal's opinion, Hitler had only postponed the final arrangements. "Weder ist Polen so schwach," Piłsudski is supposed to have said, "noch Deutschland so stark und geeint, wie er es machen will, ehe er das Risiko eines Krieges auf sich nimmt. Die Ruhepause wird uns Zeit geben, unser Leben zu gestalten—aber danach müssen wir bereit sein, uns zu verteidigen. Es bleibt uns keine andere Alternative"[4] [Poland is not so weak,... nor Germany so strong and united, as he wants to have it, before he assumes the risk of war. The break will give us time to fashion our own life—but after that we must be prepared to defend ourselves. We are left with no other alternative].

From the beginning of the establishment of the Free City of Danzig, disputes were an everyday occurrence between the Polish Government and the Danzig Senate. However, the presence in the City of Danzig of a High Commissioner was desirable from the Danzig point of view because, as Senate President Greiser wrote, "a High Commissioner—even if it is unnecessary for him to arbitrate in disputes between Danzig and Poland—by reason of his presence alone exercises a moderating influence on the course of events."[5] The Polish Government, as the Polish Foreign Minister, Beck, told his German colleague, von Neurath,[6] tolerated the League High Commissioner only because there existed no direct treaty between Poland and Germany. And as there was no such treaty, Poland would have preferred to come to some kind of agreement with Germany on Danzig. The conclusion of such an understanding, Poland pleaded, would solve the respective minority problems as well.

So on July 30 and again on August 13, 1937, the Polish Foreign Minister took the initiative and proposed in conversations with von Moltke, the German ambassador in Warsaw, that the two Governments issue a declaration that they would respect the Danzig Statute. In answer to this Moltke on September 6 told Beck that he was "authorized to state that the Führer and Reich Chancellor regarded the Danzig Statute as a reality and that he did not intend to challenge it. A public declaration to this effect, however, could not be considered."[7]

On instructions from Beck, the Polish Ambassador in Berlin, Lipski, informed Neurath that M. Beck had been misunderstood. The Polish Foreign Minister, Lipski told Neurath, did not want "still another" unilateral recognition from Germany; what Beck had in mind was a sort of bilateral declaration that would put an end to the repeated troubles over Danzig. This declaration could take the form of an exchange of notes and did not require publication. For that reason Beck had advised him (Lipski) to submit the draft of such a declaration. This read:

> The Governments of the two States contiguous to the territory of the Free City of Danzig express their agreement that in the interest of neighbouring relations between Poland and Germany, which constitute one of the essential guarantees for the preservation of peace, it is imperative to maintain the Statute which designates Danzig as the Free City, the character of the city being determined on the one hand by the Germanism (Deutschtum) of the overwhelming majority of its population, and on the other by its particular ties with Poland, the State which possesses rights in Danzig by virtue of international agreements, which forms a natural economic hinterland for the port of Danzig, and whose population possesses cultural ties with the Polish population of Danzig.[8]

Neurath told Lipski that he would have to examine this draft and the "whole matter thoroughly." The German Foreign Minister, however, made it clear to the Polish Ambassador that "for reasons of principle 'Germany' would not recognize anew the provisions of the peace treaties" and he saw no reason why Germany "should issue the Danzig Statute at the present moment."[9]

Lipski had also approached Göring and asked him to use his influence and persuade the Foreign Minister to "agree to the joint declaration proposed by Poland relative to the Danzig Statute." Göring conveyed his message, but the Foreign Minister did not "comply with this wish." "Signing the desired declaration" Neurath wrote, "would mean that the Third Reich expressly recognized the settlement of the Danzig question laid down in the peace treaty of Versailles."[10] The Führer, to whom Neurath had already reported on the matter agreed "with the above opinion." In order to leave no doubts about it with the Polish Government, the German Foreign Ministry believed that they should not delay their reply to Poland.[11]

The Polish Ambassador in Berlin was thus informed that Poland could not change the German attitude. "It involved a fundamental decision," Mackensen told Lipski, "which apart from the question of German-Polish relations, prevented us from formally reaffirming any obligation based on the Versailles Treaty."[12] Neurath himself informed Lipski again on October 18 with the German "fundamental position, namely, to make no new formal declarations of any kind regarding separate parts of the Versailles Treaty."[13] The Foreign Minister did not conceal the fact that "some day there would have to be a basic settlement of the Danzig question between Poland and us, since it would otherwise permanently disturb German-Polish relations. The only possible aim of a discussion on this matter—which, to be sure, was not all urgent—would be the restoration of German Danzig to its natural connection with the Reich, in which case extensive consideration could be given to Poland's economic interests."

The statements made by Neurath surprised Lipski, who enquired whether the Foreign Minister wanted to take up this question immediately. That was not his intention, replied the Foreign Minister. He only wished to say that Danzig was one of the questions between Poland and Germany and that it would "in due time have to be definitely settled." Lipski was requested to inform M. Beck about this.

Dissatisfied with Neurath's handling of the Polish position and unable to persuade the German Foreign Ministry to make a declaration on Danzig, Lipski requested to see the Führer.[14] The German Chancellor received the Polish Ambassador on November 5. Lipski was assured by the Führer that Germany did not intend to alter the Danzig Statute. Hitler defined his own attitude, as Lipski put it, "with great precision," formulating that there would be no changes in the legal and political position in Danzig ("an der rechtspolitischen Lage Danzigs wird nichts geändert werden"); the rights of the Polish population would be respected; and the rights of Poland in Danzig would not be impaired.[15]

The Chancellor further declared that a surprise *démarche* [diplomatic action] was out of the question. His only desire was, he said, to see the local population of Danzig given freedom to choose their own form of Government. This, the Führer thought, would avoid any possible complications or foreseeable incidents and keep particular political parties out of mischief. Lipski took cognizance of these declarations and impressed upon Hitler that the Poles had always abstained from interfering in the life of the German population and rejected "all offers coming from the opposition" in Danzig. Polish rights and interests in connection with the Free City, Lipski said, had been defined in the Polish-Danzig Convention of 1920. The Ambassador added that Danzig constituted a point where the two countries could very well collaborate: Danzig also played an important part in Polish trade. To this Hitler answered: "Danzig ist mit Polen verbunden" [Danzig is tied to Poland].

THE PROBLEM OF MINORITIES

While the question of Danzig was being discussed between Poland and Germany, the future of minority groups came to the forefront.[16] Negotiations had been carried on since the German -Polish Non-Aggression Treaty of 1934. It was decided that the two countries should come to some understanding concerning their respective minority groups. These discussions resulted in a German-Polish Joint Declaration on Minorities published on November 5, 1937.[17] In this the two Governments agreed that the treatment of the minorities was of great importance for further development of friendly and neighbourly relations between Germany and Poland, and that "in each of the two countries the well-being of the minority can be the more surely guaranteed if it is certain that the same principles will be observed in the other country." Each of the two States, "within the framework of its sovereignty," regarded the following principles as determining the treatment of the minorities.

1. Mutual respect for German and Polish nationality in itself precludes any attempt to assimilate the minority by force, to question membership in the minority, or to hinder profession of membership in the minority. In particular, no pressure of any kind will be exerted on youthful members of the minority in order to alienate them from their adherence to such minority.

2. Members of the minority shall have the right to the free use of their language in speech and in writing, in their personal and economic relations, in the press, and in public meetings.
3. The cultivation of their mother tongue and of the customs of their nationality, either in public or in private life, shall not entail any disadvantages for members of the minority.
4. The right of members of the minority to unite in associations, including those of a cultural and economic nature, shall be guaranteed.
5. The minority may maintain and establish schools in its mother tongue.
6. With respect to church life, the members of the minority shall have the right to practice their religion in their mother tongue and to organize their own churches. There shall be no interference with existing conditions in matters of faith and of charitable activities.
7. Members of the minority may not, because of their membership in such minority, be hindered or prejudiced in their choice or exercise of an occupation or economic activity. In the economic field they shall enjoy the same rights as the members of the majority nationality in the State, particularly with respect to ownership or acquisition of real property.
8. The above principles shall in no way affect the duty of members of the minority to give their undivided loyalty to the State to which they belong. These principles are laid down in an effort to assure the minority equitable living conditions and a harmonious co-existence with the majority nationality; this will contribute to progressive strengthening of friendly and neighbourly relations between Germany and Poland.[18]

The day the Minority declaration was issued,[19] Hitler received the representatives of the Polish Minority in the Reich and told them how Germany endeavoured to create a "harmonious and genuinely peaceful co-existence" of the Polish minority with the German majority in the State. The determination of the German Government, Hitler declared, to

> provide bread and work for every citizen of the Reich also extends to and is applied to the members of the Polish minority. At a time when members of the German minorities in Europe are still frequently exposed to great unemployment and great privation, the Polish minority is participating fully in the economic recovery of Germany. Similar progress has been made in the cultural activity of the Polish minority, as evidenced by the diversity of their organisations and, recently, the establishment of another Polish higher school in Germany. The Poles in Germany must, however continually, bear in mind that the protection granted them implies at the same time that they must loyally fulfil their duties towards the State and observe its laws.[20]

Hitler further warned that the protection of the German minority in Poland, "especially of its right to work and remain on its ancestral soil" would also contribute to the protection of Polish minority in Germany. The chief representative of the "Association of Poles in Germany," Dr. Kaczmarck, thanked the Chancellor and assured him of the Polish minority's "complete loyalty to the Reich and its great Führer."

Whereas Beck and Lipski were very keen to produce some kind of German declaration on Danzig, the German Foreign Minister did his best to avoid issuing any such declaration on Danzig together with the Minority Declaration. The two issues were, Neurath said, to be treated separately. However, a communiqué was published on the occasion of the publication of the Minority Declaration which expressed the Führer's satisfaction with such an agreement. The communiqué further read that at "the same time it was confirmed during the conversation that German-Polish relations would not be disturbed by the Danzig question."[21] The German Foreign Minister thought that that would suffice for the moment. They would like to see the Danzig question settled some day, but would, so Neurath said, choose the right time for it.[22]

Soon after the Minority Declaration was signed, misgivings arose in both countries regarding the maltreatment of respective minority groups. Mutual accusations and protests were made. On November 25, only twenty days after the signature of the Agreement, Bismarck, the Deputy Director of the Political Department took the opportunity to make a formal protest to the Polish Chargé d'Affaires, Prince Lubomirski, concerning unemployment in Upper Silesia where a large number of German workers had been dismissed in the eastern region. The German Government felt it necessary to notify Poland that it should put an end to such dismissals. Bismarck further suggested to the Prince that conversations between representatives of the two States should take place at regular intervals to solve such disputes as would arise while implementing the Minority Declaration.[23]

While Moltke was telling Beck that "there was already a certain feeling of disillusionment" in Berlin in view of Poland's failure to respond to Germany's desire for practical implementation of the joint declaration,[24] the Association of Poles in Germany was protesting against discrimination in the field of public instruction, in economic, social and political spheres, in the application of the new Reich Laws, as well as in the cultural and organisational activity of the Polish minority.

These accusations by the Polish minority living in Germany invited press criticism from the neighbouring country, Poland. The German Government expressed astonishment at the Polish Press, which was thought to be "exaggerating the affair in a malicious manner."[25] The German Government noted with regret that the semi-official Iskra Agency was "drawing ugly parallels with the oppression of the Polish minority in Czechoslovakia." Nevertheless the Germans were of the opinion that grievances held by the minorities should be taken out of the sphere of diplomatic and journalistic discussions and be brought to the notice of a committee of experts that would meet at regular intervals.[26]

When, on July 9, 1938, Moltke, on instructions from the new Foreign Minister, von Ribbentrop (since February 4, 1938), conveyed the German desire to work through committees, the Ambassador got the impression that the Polish Government were not too keen to show their eagerness in the matter, "probably for tactical reasons." Schliep in his conversations with Lubomirski felt that this negative attitude of Poland grew from the fear that if Poland were to enter into regular consultation on minorities, she would be following a dangerous path which might finally lead to the establishment of a new international organ. Lubomirski also informed Schliep that Poland believed members of the minority should have recourse to the competent domestic authorities.[27]

The German Foreign Ministry took it that Poland had no intention of making any change in their policy towards the German minorities and that Poland was "determined to pursue with vigour" her de-Germanizing policy. The Polish attitude towards German national groups was interpreted by the Ministry of Interior as a "frantic endeavour to appear as a great Power united in a single national State, combined with an inferiority complex."[28]

Each Government was now, it seemed, arrogating to itself the right to interpret the Minority Declaration, or even the right to persecute or torment the respective minorities.

Relations between Germany and Poland had seriously deteriorated by October 1938. Germany had been ruthless towards her Jewish minorities, many of whom were of Polish origin. Fearing a mass exodus of Polish Jews into Poland, the Polish Government, on October 15, 1938, published a decree whereby all Polish passports had to have a control stamp in order to remain valid. Passports which did not bear such stamps no longer authorized entry into the Polish territory. This meant, the Germans concluded, that nearly 70,000 Polish Jews had to be tolerated permanently in the Reich territory.[29] On October 26, the German Embassy in Warsaw demanded that the Polish Government should admit holders of Polish passports that did not bear the control stamp. Otherwise, the Embassy notified, the German Government "would find itself compelled, as a matter of precaution to expel all Polish Jews from Reich territory on very short notice." At the same time the Foreign Ministry in Berlin instructed the alien control authorities to issue immediate orders on a large scale to Polish Jews "prohibiting further residence in Reich territory." The Polish passport decree was to come into force on October

30; the German Government set October 21 as the last date for leaving the German territory. On October 28 and 29 about 15,000 Polish Jews from all over Germany were rounded up, taken into custody and brought to the Polish border for deportation. In spite of the fact that the Polish decree came into effect on October 30, the Polish border police refused to receive the Polish Jews. The Germans, however, surreptitiously succeeded in pushing some 12,000 Jews into Poland: "über die grüne Grenze" [across the green border (running through nature in-between official border posts)], as the Germans called it. The Polish Government issued instructions to expel *Reichsdeutsche* [Germans (not Austrians)] immediately in reprisal. The deportation of the Jews from Germany was then temporarily discontinued because of—as the Germans put it—the "brutal Polish countermeasures."[30]

The Polish measures were regarded as intolerable by the German Government. Hitler is supposed to have said that he did not intend to put up any longer with the conduct of his Eastern neighbour towards his countrymen.[31] Negotiations were resumed again. These resulted in an agreement which was put into force on January 24, 1939. This agreement provided that the expelled Polish Jews were to return temporarily to Reich territory in order to take away personal property or to liquidate other assets without hindrance. The proceeds were to be transferred "through a special foreign exchange account to be set up by the two Governments." It was also agreed that the temporary returnees in Germany were not to exceed 1,000 "at any one time and the opportunity for such temporary return" was to expire on July 31, 1939. Poland was forced to take back what Weizsäcker called, "Polish property—and that is what the Polish Jews were...."[32] The Reichsführer-SS was to see that the very few "Stateless" Jews[33] still in the Reich, left Reich territory through action of the alien control police.[34]

NOTES

1. For a clear expression of German views on this question see: Walther Recke, *Die polnische Frage als Problem der europäischen Politik* (Berlin: Verlag von Georg Stilke, 1927); Fritz Prinzhorn, *Danzig-Polen-Korridor und Grenzgebiete* (Danzig: F. Prinzhorn, 1932); Hermann Rauschning, *Deutsche und Polen* (Danzig: Danziger Gesellschaft zum Studium Polens, 1934); Hans Rothfels, "Der Vertrag von Versailles und der deutsche Osten," *Berliner Monatshefte* 12 (1934): 12; Stanislaw J. Paprocki, *Polen und das Minderheitenproblem* (Warschau: Institut zur Erforschung der Minderheitsfragen, 1935); Hans Rothfels, "*Ostraum, Preussentum und Reichsgedanke. Historische Abhandlungen, Vorträge und Reden* (Leipzig: Hinrichs, 1935); Otto Bail, *Die Völkerrechtliche Lage der Freien Stadt Danzig* (PhD diss., Ruck: Quakenbrück, 1939).

And for a more recent and brilliant study of the problem see Richard Breyer, *Das Deutsche Reich und Polen, 1932–1937: Aussenpolitik und Volksgruppenfragen* (Würzburg: Holzner-Verlag, 1955), 15. According to Breyer, "Die Praxis von Versailles liess es nicht zu von einem gerechten und dauerhaften Frieden zu sprechen. Überall dort, wo national strittige Gebiete an der Ostgrenze des Deutschen Reiches bestanden hatten, ist in Versailles die Grenze zugunsten Polens gezogen worden. Darüber hinaus wurden auch Gebiete nur aus strategischen oder wirtschaftlichen Gründen abgetrennt. Auf diese Weise wurde das territoriale Problem wie es sich vor allem um Danzig, den durch die Abtrennung Westpreussens geschaffenen Korridor und das geteilte Oberschlesien konzentrierte, zum politischen Streitobjekt" [The application of Versailles did not allow speaking of a just and lasting peace. Wherever there had existed nationally contested regions along the Eastern border of the German Reich, in Versailles the border was drawn in favor of Poland. Beyond that territories were separated as well solely for strategic or economic reasons. This meant that the territorial problem concentrated primarily around Danzig, the corridor created by the separation of West Prussia and the partitioned Upper Silesia, became a political controversy]. Translations for the non-English text have been provided by Elfa Halloway and Hiam Halawi.

2. Hans Roos, *Polen und Europa; Studien zur Geschichte und Politik, 1931–1939* (thesis, Tübingen, Germany: Mohr, 1957), 118.

3. Declaration concerning the relations between Poland and Germany signed in Berlin, January 26, 1934. Official translation issued by the Polish Embassy in London, Royal Institute of International Affairs, *Documents on International Affairs, 1933 to 1939* (London: Oxford University Press, 1940), 424–25.

4. Quoted in Roos, *Polen und Europa*, 118.

5. E. L. Woodward and Rohan Butler, eds. "Greiser to Shepherd, Shepherd to Halifax," in *Documents on British Foreign Policy, 1919–1939*, Third Series, Volume 3, *1938-9* (London: H. M. Stationery Office, 1950), No. 514, enclosure.

6. German Foreign Ministry, *Documents on German Foreign Policy, 1918–1945*, Series D, Volume 5, *Poland, the Balkans, Latin America, the Smaller Powers, June 1937–March 1939*, (London: H. M. Stationery Office, 1953), No. 28.

7. German Foreign Ministry, *German Foreign Policy*, Series D, Volume 5, No. 1, n. 2.

8. Memorandum by Neurath, September 11, 1937, in German Foreign Ministry, *German Foreign Policy*, Series D, Volume 5, No. 1.

9. Memorandum by Neurath, September 11, 1937, in German Foreign Ministry, *German Foreign Policy*, Series D, Volume 5, No. 1.

10. October 1, 1937, in German Foreign Ministry, *German Foreign Policy*, Series D, Volume 5, No. 6.

11. Mackensen, the State Secretary to the Embassy in Poland, October 4, 1937, in German Foreign Ministry, *German Foreign Policy*, Series D, Volume 5, No. 7.

12. Memorandum by Mackensen, October 7, 1937, in German Foreign Ministry, *German Foreign Policy*, Series D, Volume 5, No. 11.

13. Memorandum by Neurath, October 18, 1937, in German Foreign Ministry, *German Foreign Policy*, Series D, Volume 5, No. 13.

14. Memorandum by Neurath, November 6, 1937, in German Foreign Ministry, *German Foreign Policy*, Series D, Volume 5, No. 19.

15. Republic of Poland, *Official Documents Concerning Polish-German and Polish-Soviet Relations, 1933–1939* (*Polish White Book*) (London: Ministry for Foreign Affairs for the Republic of Poland, 1939), No. 34 (hereafter referred to and cited as "Polish White Book").

16. For a detailed description of the Polish-German minority problems, see Breyer, *Das Deutsche Reich.*

17. German Foreign Ministry, *German Foreign Policy*, Series D, Volume 5, No. 18; Republic of Poland, "Polish White Book," No. 32.

18. German Foreign Ministry, *German Foreign Policy*, Series D, Volume 5, No. 18; Republic of Poland, "Polish White Book," No. 32.

19. November 5, 1937.

20. German Foreign Ministry, *German Foreign Policy*, Series D, Volume 5, No. 18, 25.

21. Earlier on November 2, 1937, Lipski had proposed a revision of the communiqué which, accepted by Neurath, read: "At the same time it was possible to confirm during the conversation that the two Governments were also in full agreement in their attitude on Danzig affairs and that German-Polish relations would not be disturbed by this question." This was dropped out of the final version. The State Secretary had received the Polish Ambassador on November 4 and given him a negative decision (German Foreign Ministry, *German Foreign Policy*, Series D, Volume 5, No. 18, 26, n. 1).

22. Memorandum by Neurath, October 23, 1937, in German Foreign Ministry, *German Foreign Policy*, Series D, Volume 5, No. 16.

23. Neurath had, on November 4, 1937, handed an *aide-mémoire* to the Polish Ambassador, outlining proposals for such meetings (Memorandum by the Foreign Minister, November 25, 1937, in German Foreign Ministry, *German Foreign Policy*, Series D, Volume 5, No. 23, 29, n. 2).

24. German Foreign Ministry, *German Foreign Policy*, Series D, Volume 5, No. 23.

25. Memorandum by Schliep, Head of the Political Division, V; in German Foreign Ministry, *German Foreign Policy*, Series D, Volume 5, No. 39.

26. Ribbentrop to Moltke, June 29, 1938, in German Foreign Ministry, *German Foreign Policy*, Series D, Volume 5, No. 44.

27. Memorandum by Schliep, in German Foreign Ministry, *German Foreign Policy*, Series D, Volume 5, No. 27. Lubomirski had expressed these fears as early as in January 1938. One cannot tell how valid these fears were. Poland could have later in July (when Moltke proposed new lines) given Germany the benefit of the doubt and stretched her hand of co-operation. For, conversation among experts did not mean the establishment of an international organ, nor did it imply interference in the domestic affairs of the respective countries. These informal discussions could have had favorable results at least in eliminating political tension, rioting and the newspaper war, the effect of which was to incite the minorities of both countries in later months.

28. German Foreign Ministry, *Documents on German Foreign Policy, 1918–1945*, Series D, Volume 6, *The Last Months of Peace, March–August, 1939* (London: H. M. Stationery Office, 1956), No. 125.

29. The Reichsführer-SS to the Chief of the Reich Chancellery, October 29, 1938, in German Foreign Ministry, *German Foreign Policy*, Series D, Volume 5, No. 91.

30. Memorandum by Reifegerste, November 11, 1938, in German Foreign Ministry, *German Foreign Policy*, Series D, Volume 5, No. 98.

31. Note by Twardowski, November 12, 1938, in German Foreign Ministry, *German Foreign Policy*, Series D, Volume 5, No. 99.

32. Memorandum by Weizsäcker, November 8, 1938, in German Foreign Ministry, *German Foreign Policy*, Series D, Volume 5, No. 95.

33. The number of Polish Jews in Germany in 1933 was some 70,000, and in February 1939 about 5,000 to 6,000.

34. The Reichsführer-SS to the Chief of the Reich Chancellery, February 3, 1939, in German Foreign Ministry, *German Foreign Policy*, Series D, Volume 5, No. 127.

Chapter 2

The Teschen Problem, September–October 1938

Although the minority question and the treatment of it left Poland and Germany bitter towards each other, the negotiations over Danzig were momentarily overshadowed by Germany's preoccupation with the Sudeten problem, and the immediate Polish interests in the Teschen territory. Poland wanted to annex districts inhabited by the people of Polish origin in Czechoslovakia, at the very time that Germany was advancing her demands on Sudetenland. Since Poland was not invited to participate in the Munich Conference, the Polish Government decided to proceed on their own to settle their territorial claims. Poland felt that she needed Germany's moral support. Poland counted on it and in fact got it.

Hitler defined Czechoslovakia as a "purely artificial structure which had been called into being at the time for reasons of political expediency, without regard for the wrongs done to other countries." In his conversations with Chamberlain at Godesberg on the afternoon of September 22, 1938, the German Chancellor made a strong plea for the Polish and the Hungarian claims on Czechoslovakia. Millions of Germans, Hitler told Chamberlain, had been handed over to Czechoslovakia against their express wishes and in contradiction to all historical traditions; a million Slovaks, and hundreds of thousands of Hungarians and Poles had likewise been incorporated by the Czech State. The Poles and the Hungarians had told him, Hitler argued, that in no circumstances could these minorities remain in Czechoslovakia. Although he was, Hitler said, speaking in the first place for the Germans, he felt it his duty to remind the British Prime Minister of the wishes of other nationalities within Czechoslovakia and added that all these minority groups had the "sincere sympathy of the German Reich and that peace could not be established in Central Europe until the claims of all these nationalities had been settled."[1] Hitler was not, so he claimed, even prepared to join in the guarantee of the Czechoslovak State: A guarantee could be given only when all Germany's neighbours had done so. Germany could not, Hitler contended, even sign a non-aggression pact with Czechoslovakia as long as her problems with Poland and Hungary remained unsolved and because of Germany's friendly relations with these two countries, Hitler could not, he said, afford to "stab them in the back" by concluding a non-aggression treaty with Czechoslovakia.

This attitude of the German Chancellor was fully appreciated by the Polish Government and the Polish public.[2]

Poland put forward an argument that she was entitled to similar treatment in the Teschen district of Czechoslovakia as was accorded the Germans in Sudetenland: A plebiscite for the Polish minority in Teschen. If no such possibility was foreseen a direct annexation of this territory by the Polish Government would be contemplated.[3] Before taking any such steps, the Polish Foreign Minister saw to it that Poland could count on Germany's benevolent attitude.[4] The German Foreign Ministry on their part left no doubt that they fully sympathized with the Poles and understood the Polish standpoint. Thereupon the Polish Ambassador in Berlin was given the following statement by Ribbentrop:[5]

1. We had complete understanding for the Polish viewpoint;
2. We hoped that military action would not become necessary; the condition for this, it seemed to us, was that Prague should accommodate itself immediately to the Polish demands and quickly comply with the wishes of the Poles;
3. In case of an armed conflict between Poland and Czechoslovakia, we would naturally take a benevolent attitude;
4. Should the Soviet Union proceed against Poland militarily, which I think is out of the question, however, a completely new situation would arise for Germany in the whole Czechoslovak problem.[6]

The "loyal treatment" accorded the Polish interests by Germany led to expressed gratification by the Polish Foreign Minister.[7] But such treatment also gave rise to fears that Hitler was likely to want to lay Poland under an obligation by "espousing the cause of the Polish minority."[8] The very thought of this was distasteful to the Polish Government, who hesitated at granting another victory to Hitler. The Polish Government, they said, wanted the question of the Polish minority in Czechoslovakia to be settled parallel with that of the Sudeten Germans but independent of Germany.[9] Thus to realize her ambitions Poland also sought British support. The Polish Embassy in London tried to impress upon the Foreign Office that Poland should take the opportunity of strengthening herself and if she failed to importune her right then Polish ambitions would be discomfited by Germany later. These arguments invited a sympathetic response from Sir H. Kennard, His Majesty's Ambassador in Warsaw. The British Ambassador also feared that if Poland obtained no "territorial advantage" and if the Great Powers guaranteed the new Czechoslovak frontiers "against future revision, will not Poland feel, far from gaining, she has actually been the loser by such a settlement? This might involve serious deterioration of Anglo-Polish relations."[10] Kennard ventured to draw the British Government's attention to what the Ambassador thought was of "immediate" and of "future" concern. It had appeared to Kennard, though he said he had "no concrete evidence of such an intention," that, were Germany to cede Sudetenland while Polish claims to equal treatment were ignored, the British Government might be faced with a *fait accompli* [an action already completed] by Poland. If the general impression prevailed that Czechoslovakia was to be sacrificed by France and Great Britain, it was possible, Kennard contended, that Beck could advance this argument as a justification for his conciliatory policy toward Germany, since France and Great Britain were believed to be untrustworthy allies.[11]

The Foreign Office responded quickly to Kennard's observation and made it known that the guarantee offered by His Majesty's Government to Czechoslovakia was a guarantee against "unprovoked aggression," but did not "prejudice the treatment of the other minorities problems, except that that treatment must not be by way of unprovoked aggression."[12]

On September 21, the Polish Ambassador in London, Count Raczynski, called on Halifax and reminded the Foreign Secretary of the need for equality of treatment of the Polish minority and reiterated the demand for the return to Poland of the territory inhabited by the Polish minority on the same terms as had been accepted for the Sudetens. The Polish Ambassador argued that the crisis in Central Europe could not be "finally settled" without the solution of the minority problems in Czechoslovakia.[13] Raczynski further emphasized that "in the event of this point of view not being accepted, the Polish Government would, to their great regret, be obliged to reserve their attitude with regard to their eventual collaboration in the proposed settlement by the problems in question."[14] Halifax assured the Count that His Majesty's Government was fully aware of the situation and hoped that Colonel Beck and the Polish Government would be content with the British assurances. Such questions, the Foreign Secretary added, could be raised "at the appropriate moment" when they "would no doubt receive proper consideration." Lord Halifax also referred to Article 19 of the League Charter, which provided for the revision of the treaties. To this the Ambassador retorted that that was "equivalent to shelving it." Raczynski complained that nothing had happened under Article 19 and he had reasons to believe that nothing was likely to happen in the near future. If that was how the Ambassador viewed the situation, the Foreign Secretary told Raczynski, there were, then, only two ways by which such problems could be solved: one by war, which was a "very double-edged weapon," and the other by negotiations. Halifax very much hoped that Poland "would not further aggravate the dangerous situation in Europe." The British Government also informed Poland that they were, at that moment, concentrating all their efforts on the problem of the Sudeten minority in Czechoslovakia on the solution of which, the British Government believed, depended the "issue of peace or war in Europe, an issue which must be of primary concern to all European States, and particularly to those contiguous to Czechoslovakia."[15]

While the Polish Ambassador was making his representation at the Foreign Office, the Polish Foreign Ministry, on September 21, sent a note to the Czechoslovak Government demanding equal treatment for the Polish minority and threatening that Poland would regulate her action according to the nature of the reply received. This note, as Kennard reported, was followed by the mass demonstrations for the recovery of Teschen in Warsaw, and the movement of troops along the Polish-Czechoslovak frontier.[16]

His Majesty's Government learned "with regret that the Polish (Hungarian) Government should have found it necessary to take special military measures which appear to have no other object than to intimidate the Czechoslovak Government." "His Majesty's Government cannot agree," Kennard was instructed at once to inform the Polish Government, "that there is any justification for such a policy of intimidation and they sincerely hope that the Polish (Hungarian) Government will not persist in it and above all that they will not carry it to the point where it would involve them in an actual act of aggression against the Czechoslovak State."[17]

The British remonstrance did not have any effect upon Beck's policies. The Polish Foreign Minister informed the British Government that the matter concerned only Prague and Warsaw, and no one else.[18] Beck refused to give the assurance that Britain had requested. He would not, Beck said to Kennard, "have his hands tied in this way and Germans given preferential treatment over Poles."[19] Beck also answered the British protest against intimidating the Czechoslovak Government in these words:

> With regard to certain measures of security which have been taken by the Polish Government, I do not consider it useful to make these a subject of discussion, since the Polish Government must judge for themselves of the advisability of measures to be taken for safeguarding legitimate Polish interests.
> I should also like to emphasize that among European Powers, including United Kingdom, Poland is the last to take indispensable measures of a military character.[20]

President Beneš of the Czechoslovak Republic, had, in answer to the Polish note of September 21, written a letter dated September 22 to the Polish President Moscicki, expressing his Government's sincere desire for an everlasting friendship between the two countries and that the Czechoslovak Government was prepared to accept the principle of rectification of frontiers.[21] Accordingly therefore, the Czechoslovak Minister for Foreign Affairs, M. Krafta, formally offered the solemn assurance that "rectification of the frontiers and subsequent territory transfer may take place whatever the international situation," and proposed: (a) that districts "in question shall be divided according to proportion of Polish and Czech inhabitants"; (b) the composition of a Commission of Poles and Czechs "qui élaborevait la procédure de détail sur la base de ce principe" [that would develop the procedure and details on the basis of this principle]. This Commission would meet on October 5: "cette commission réglerait notamment encore les question concernant l'option des habitants, les déplacements et échanges réciproques de population, ainsi que toutes les question économiques et financières qui en dependent" [this commission would mainly settle the questions concerning the residents' option, the movement and mutual exchanges of populations, as well as all the economic and financial matters depending on it]. The Commission would finish its work by the 30th of October; (c) "il sevait immédiatement fixé la date à laquelle doit s'effectuer la remise des territoires. Cette date sevait fixeé en determinant les limites extrême: la date la plus proche possible et la dernière date possible" [the date on which the territories would be handed over would be fixed immediately. This date would be fixed by determining the outermost limits: the nearest date possible and the possible farthest date].

A communiqué was to be issued declaring that agreement had been reached on the rectification of the frontiers. The note ended with the hope that such a settlement would be lasting and without bitterness.[22]

The Czechoslovak Government believed their proposals to be considerate and reasonable. The Poles did not find them so, since, as they said, the proposals did not mention Teschen explicitly or the ceding of this territory unconditionally. The Polish Government, therefore, sent a humiliating ultimatum on September 30. The Czech plan, it said, was entirely "insufficient and dilatory" and since "le Gouvernement polonais ne peu plus accorder de confiance aux déclarations faites au nom de la République Tchécoslovaque" [the Polish government can no longer trust declarations issued in the name of the Czech Republic]. Poland categorically demanded:

1. Evacuation of a certain defined area within 24 hours as from mid-day October 1.
2. The cession of remainder of districts of Teschen Frysztat within ten days starting from the same date.

3. Public utilities and communications in evacuated areas to be left intact and defensive works to be disarmed.
4. Question of plebiscite in other areas to be subsequently agreed between the two Governments with the possible participation of third parties.
5. Persons of Polish tongue born in districts of Teschen Frysztat to be immediately released from military service and all political prisoners of Polish origin to be released.
6. A reply accepting or rejecting demands to be given by mid-day October 1. Should reply be not forthcoming or contain refusal Polish Government will hold the Czechoslovak Government solely responsible for the consequences.[23]

Two days before the Polish ultimatum was delivered, Beneš had personally proposed (September 28) to the Polish Minister in Prague that Czechoslovakia "was prepared to declare immediately and on principle its free will to cede territory to Poland, but this secession could only be affected after all modalities connected with it had been settled by negotiation. In these negotiations Poland ought to take into consideration vital Czechoslovak interests which are now in the balance. Otherwise the balance would be destroyed, on which both countries intended to base their future good-neighbourly relationship. An arrangement as demanded with such haste by Poland would be nothing else but a dictate to be imposed by force."[24]

Even these promises did not stop the Polish Government from sending the ultimatum to Prague.

M. Beck refused the British Government's offer of mediation "as it was too late."[25] It indeed was. By mid-day October 1, the Czechoslovak Government had accepted Polish demands in their entirety.

Whereas the British, the French and the Italian Missions had addressed protests to the Warsaw Government, the Germans had followed strictly the policy of "benevolent attitude." Poland had, Moltke reported, for the moment proved that she could by her own actions force a solution on the Czechs within twelve hours. By her actions, the German Ambassador noted, Poland even pretended that she had helped Germany realize her hopes in Czechoslovakia. German enterprise in Sudetenland, Beck told Moltke, would have been impossible "if Poland by her neutrality policy had not precluded any military operation on the part of Soviet Russia."[26]

Germany had no special interest in Teschen, though she showed her concern wherever there was a *Volksdeutscher* [an ethnic German]. Even if Hitler was conniving at the Polish ultimatum to Czechoslovakia, he was, he said, doing it as a favour to Poland. He did not want, the Chancellor told Ribbentrop, to "haggle with the Poles about every single city but would be generous towards those who were modest in their demands."[27] The places where Polish-German interests clashed were Slovakia and Carpatho-Ukraine. The German Ambassador Moltke had the feeling that Beck coquetted with the temptation of establishing an independent Slovakia, with Poland serving as its tutelary authority.[28] The Polish Foreign Minister had told Moltke that the linguistic similarity between Poland and Slovakia was greater than that between any other two Slavic nations, and Beck had therefore contended that the Slovaks had "a very special confidence in Poland." Moltke was also told, that Slovaks had developed their own nationality in the past twenty years and that they would ask for "nothing better than to retain this acquisition; whether within the framework of the Czechoslovak State or in some other way was a matter of less importance to them."[29] "It struck me," wrote Moltke, "that the otherwise usual reference to the fact that Poland had no aspirations south of the Carpathians was lacking this time."[30]

Beck had a solution for the Carpatho-Ukraine as well. The Polish Foreign Minister told Moltke that the annexation of this territory by Hungary was the right solution: The Polish political circles believed the creation of a common frontier with Hungary to be very vital. The realization of such an aim would have, in the eyes of M. Beck, established an "effective barrier" against the threat of Bolshevism.[31] Poland, therefore, favoured an autonomous Carpatho-Ukraine "associated" with Hungary. Carpatho-Ukraine had been, so the Poles thought, the seat of communist activity against Poland. Therefore the Polish Government believed that the association of this territory with Prague meant absence of complete authority in this area, but annexation with the Hungarians would bring peace and tranquility.[32] Not only that: M. Beck regarded the inclusion of Carpatho-Ukraine in Czechoslovakia unjustified either "geopolitically, ethnographically or economically." The Polish Foreign Minister ruled out plebiscite in this region because, he told Moltke, the people were illiterate.

The German Ambassador in Warsaw carefully noted Beck's concern in Slovakia and the Carpatho-Ukraine region. Moltke advised the Foreign Ministry in Berlin that Beck was not so keen on a common frontier with the Hungarians or so scrupulous in keeping the Bolshevists out, as he was in preventing a violent resurgence of the Polish Ukrainians. Poland, Moltke reported, would do anything to oppose the formation of Greater Ukraine or "the new centre of crystallization sought by the Ukrainians." Moltke described the Polish fears that, if the Carpatho-Ukrainians would remain under Czech influence, they might, later, surrender to German influence. This would place Germany in a position to intervene at her discretion. The very thought of it looked damaging to Polish interests and an advantage to Germany's strategical position. The Ambassador gathered that Poland was thus faced with the existing Soviet penetration and the new German sphere of influence on Poland's southern frontier. German policy towards the

Ukrainians, Moltke concluded, was therefore followed with great distrust by the Government in Warsaw.[33]

Ribbentrop told Lipski that Germany had understanding for the Polish wishes. The Foreign Minister, however, remarked that he thought a favourable arrangement on the Slovak and the Carpatho-Ukrainian questions could be found, if a general settlement between Poland and Germany on more important problems was reached.[34]

NOTES

1. For the Minutes of the conversation between the Reich Chancellor and Mr. Chamberlain on September 22, 1938, see German Foreign Ministry, *Documents on German Foreign Policy, 1918–1945*, Series D, Volume 2, *Germany and Czechoslovakia, 1937–1938*, (London: H. M. Stationery Office, 1950), No. 562.

2. Beck to Moltke, October 1, 1938, German Foreign Ministry, *Documents on German Foreign Policy, 1918–1945*, Series D, Volume 5, *Poland, the Balkans, Latin America, the Smaller Powers, June 1937–March 1939*, (London: H. M. Stationery Office, 1953), No. 54.

3. On September 19, 1938, the Polish Ambassador in London, Count Raczynski, called at the Foreign Office, to deliver a communication which according to the Polish Government was to be "considered as a very formal and serious *démarche* [diplomatic step]." The text of the message ran as follows: "Les informations que le Gouvernement polonaise reçoit sur le règlement projeté du problème des Sudètes par voie d'une nouvelle délimitation des frontiers au lieu d'un plebiscite peut-être inopportun en l'instance place (*sic*) de Gouvernement devant la nécessité de soulever une demande analogue par rapport aux territoires polonais en Silésie de Cieszyn. Le Gouvernement polonais est, d'avis que la crise actuelle en Tchécoslovaquie ne pourrait être résolue par un traitment trop restreint. L'exclusion des demandes de la Pologne aurait comme suite une tension entre la Pologne et la Tchécoslovaquie" [The information received by the Polish government regarding the intended settlement of the Sudetenland problem by means of a new delimitation of frontiers, instead of a plebiscite, might be inappropriate given the circumstances. It forces the government to make a similar request with respect to the Polish territories in Silesia of Teschen. The Polish government is of the opinion that the current crisis in Czechoslovakia cannot be resolved in such a restricted manner. The exclusion of the demands of Poland would cause, as a result, tension between Poland and Czechoslovakia] (text in original: E. L. Woodward and Rohan Butler, eds., *Documents on British Foreign Policy, 1919–1939*, Third Series, Volume 3, *1938-9* [London: H. M. Stationery Office, 1950], No. 11, enclosure).

4. Polish ultimatum to Czechoslovakia was sent on September 30.

5. Memorandum by Ribbentrop, October 1, 1938, in German Foreign Ministry, *German Foreign Policy, 1918–1945*, Series D. Volume 5, *Poland, the Balkans, Latin America, the Smaller Powers, June 1937–March 1939* (London: H. M. Stationery Office, 1953), No. 55.

6. With regard to Clause 4, Moltke told Beck, "in case of Russian intervention we would likewise adopt a benevolent attitude, but in that event an entirely new situation would confront us" (German Foreign Ministry, *German Foreign Policy*, Series D, Volume 5, No. 55, n. 1). The Italian Ambassador in Warsaw did not use the same language as Moltke. Ciano's instructions were that the Italian Government did not expect that Poland would resort to force just because of a few days. Ciano to Ribbentrop, October 1, 1938 (Memorandum by Ribbentrop, in German Foreign Ministry, *German Foreign Policy*, Series D, Volume 5, No. 55).

7. Beck to Moltke, October 1, 1938, in German Foreign Ministry, *German Foreign Policy*, Series D, Volume 5, No. 54.

8. Count Michalowski, First Secretary of the Polish Embassy in London to Mr. Strang, September 21, 1938, in Woodward and Butler, *British Foreign Policy*, Third Series, Volume 3, No. 21.

9. Woodward and Butler, *British Foreign Policy*, Third Series, Volume 3.

10. Kennard to Halifax, September 20, 1938, in Woodward and Butler, *British Foreign Policy*, Third Series, Volume 3, No. 13.

11. Woodward and Butler, *British Foreign Policy*, Third Series, Volume 3.

12. Halifax to Norton (Warsaw) and to Gascoigne (Budapest), September 21, 1938, in Woodward and Butler, *British Foreign Policy*, Third Series, Volume 3, No. 19.

13. At this very period, the Hungarians were making their claims on the Czechoslovakian territory. The Hungarian Government found their best friends in the Polish Foreign Ministry. The Ministry gave vent to the Hungarian wishes every time the Polish Government complained about their own minorities.

14. Note handed by the Polish Ambassador to the Secretary of State, September 21, 1938, in Woodward and Butler, *British Foreign Policy*, Third Series, Volume 3, No. 20, enclosure 1.

15. Halifax to Raczynski, September 20, 1938, in Woodward and Butler, *British Foreign Policy*, Third Series, Volume 3, No. 2, enclosure 2.

16. Kennard to Halifax, September 22, 1938, in Woodward and Butler, *British Foreign Policy*, Third Series, Volume 3, No. 22, also Nos. 32 and 33.

17. Halifax to Kennard (Warsaw) and Knox (Budapest), September 22, 1938, in E. L. Woodward and Rohan Butler, eds., *Documents on British Foreign Policy, 1919–1939*, Third Series, Volume 2, *1938* (London: H. M. Stationery Office, 1947), No. 1024.

18. Beck to Kennard, Kennard to Halifax, September 23, 1938, in Woodward and Butler, *British Foreign Policy*, Third Series, Volume 3, No. 35.

19. Woodward and Butler, *British Foreign Policy*, Third Series, Volume 3.

20. Woodward and Butler, *British Foreign Policy*, Third Series, Volume 3, No. 34. For exchange of letters between Kennard and Beck, see *British Foreign Policy*, Third Series, Volume 3, No. 45, enclosures 1 and 2. Kennard also reported that Beck had informed him that the "Soviet Government had informed Polish Chargé d'Affaires in Moscow that in accordance with Article 2 of Russo-Polish Pact of Non-Aggression the Soviet would consider themselves at liberty to denounce the Pact in the event of Poland attacking Czechoslovakia. The Polish Government have replied to this threat by stating that they are the sole judge of any action which they may think it necessary

to take and that they can read the text of their engagements just as well as Soviet" (Kennard to Halifax, September 23, 1938, in Woodward and Butler, *British Foreign Policy*, Third Series, Volume 3, No. 35). The Polish Chargé d'Affaires in Moscow had also "in strict confidence" informed Schulenburg, the German Ambassador in Moscow, about such a Soviet *démarche* and the Polish reply (Schulenburg to the Foreign Ministry, September 23, 1938, in German Foreign Ministry, *German Foreign Policy*, Series D, Volume 2, No. 582).

21. Mr. Newton (Prague) was given by the Prague Government in "strict confidence" the text of personal letters exchanged between Beneš and Moscicki; Newton to Halifax, September 28, 1938, in Woodward and Butler, *British Foreign Policy*, Third Series, Volume 3, No. 60.

22. Czechoslovak Minister for Foreign Affairs to the Polish Minister in Prague, September 30, 1938, published in original, in Woodward and Butler, *British Foreign Policy*, Third Series, Volume 3, No. 101, Annex. I.

23. Newton to Halifax, October 1, 1938, in Woodward and Butler, *British Foreign Policy*, Third Series, Volume 3, No. 89. For full text in the original, see *British Foreign Policy*, Third Series, Volume 3, No. 101, Annex II.

24. Quoted from the *aide-mémoire* handed by the Czechoslovak Minister in London to the Foreign Office, September 29, 1938, in Woodward and Butler, *British Foreign Policy*, Third Series, Volume 3, no. 71.

25. Kennard to Halifax, October 1, 1938, in Woodward and Butler, *British Foreign Policy*, Third Series, Volume 3, No. 93.

26. Moltke to the Foreign Ministry, October 6, 1938, in German Foreign Ministry, *German Foreign Policy*, Series D, Volume 5, No. 64.

27. Memorandum by Hewel, October 5, 1938, in German Foreign Ministry, *German Foreign Policy*, Series D, Volume 5, No. 62.

28. Moltke to the Foreign Ministry, October 27, 1938, in German Foreign Ministry, *German Foreign Policy*, Series D, Volume 5, No. 87. Moltke had requested comment on a report of the Prague Legation that a Slovak Deputy, Sidor, was working as Beck's agent to "persuade the Slovaks to declare their independence from Prague and then to join Poland in a personal union" (*German Foreign Policy*, Series D, Volume 5, No. 1).

29. Moltke to the Foreign Ministry, July 1, 1938, in German Foreign Ministry, *German Foreign Policy*, Series D, Volume 2, No. 277.

30. Moltke to the Foreign Ministry, in German Foreign Ministry, *German Foreign Policy*, Series D, Volume 2.

31. Moltke to the Foreign Ministry, October 19, 1938, in German Foreign Ministry, *German Foreign Policy*, Series D, Volume 5, No. 76.

32. Lipski to Woermann: Memorandum by Woermann, October 22, 1938, in German Foreign Ministry, *German Foreign Policy*, Series D, Volume 5, No. 80.

33. Moltke to the Foreign Ministry, October 19, 1938, in German Foreign Ministry, *German Foreign Policy*, Series D, Volume 5, No. 76.

34. Memorandum by Hewel, October 24, 1938, in German Foreign Ministry, *German Foreign Policy*, Series D, Volume 5, No. 81.

Chapter 3

The Stage Is Set

FURTHER EXCHANGE OF VIEWS ON DANZIG AND THE CORRIDOR

The Czechoslovak crisis out of the way, Ribbentrop, on October 24, 1938, invited Lipski to Berchtesgaden to discuss the "large general problem" which the Reich Foreign Minister "wished to broach in strict confidence as between only *Lipski, Beck and himself.*" Ribbentrop explained that he thought that "it was time to arrive at a general settlement of all possible points of friction between Germany and Poland. This would be a culmination of the work started by Marshal Piłsudski and the Führer." The Foreign Minister compared German relations with Italy "where for the sake of a general settlement and out of deep perception the Führer had renounced the South Tyrol," etc. etc. "Such an arrangement," Ribbentrop explained, "was desirable also with Poland and for Poland, and was in line with the Führer's policy of achieving clarity" in Germany's relations with her neighbours: Here it was "necessary to speak with Poland first of all about Danzig, as one part of a large settlement between the two nations. Danzig was German—had always been German and would always remain German." The Foreign Minister then proposed a solution on the following terms:

1. The Free State of Danzig would revert to the German Reich.
2. An extra-territorial *Reichsautobahn* belonging to Germany and likewise an extra-territorial, multiple-track railroad would be laid through the Corridor.
3. Similarly, Poland would receive in the Danzig area an extra-territorial road or *Autobahn*, a railroad, and a free port.
4. Poland would receive a guarantee of a market for her goods in the Danzig area.
5. The two nations would recognize their common boundaries (guarantee) or each other's territories.
6. The German-Polish treaty would be extended 10 to 25 years.

7. Poland would accede to the Anti-Comintern Pact.
8. The two countries would add a consultation clause to their treaty.¹

Lipski took "cognizance" of these proposals. Although he would have to speak with Beck first, he wanted, Lipski said to Ribbentrop, to express himself then on the Danzig problem in these terms: "It was wrong to view Danzig as a product of Versailles, like the Saar region for instance. It was necessary to trace the historical and geographical origin of Danzig in order to obtain the proper perspective on the question. Danzig was a problem handed down from the Middle Ages. From time immemorial it had been the city of the mouth of the Vistula, the outlet to the sea for the hinterland on the Vistula, Poland, with her 35,000,000 people. Danzig had risen from comparative insignificance when Poland rose again after the war. Thus the City was for Poland almost a symbol. Poland had always refused to meddle in the internal political problems of Danzig, and had repeatedly demonstrated this when the parties had appealed to Poland for help against the N.S.D.A.P. Poland had viewed this as a German domestic concern and had always recognised the German character of Danzig." Lipski therefore did not "consider an *Anschluss* possible, however, if only—and principally—for reasons of domestic policy. Beck could never prevail upon the people to accept it."

The Foreign Minister thereupon advised Lipski not to answer him now but to "think all these things over and speak with Beck about them as soon as possible." "After all," Ribbentrop added, "one should not exclude a certain reciprocity in the consideration of these matters. For the Führer's final recognition of the Corridor was also not easy from the standpoint of domestic policy. Moreover, it was necessary to take a long-range view of the matter—and Danzig was in the last analysis German and would always remain so."

The Polish Ambassador received instructions² from Warsaw and he read them to Ribbentrop on November 19: "Foreign Minister Beck was of the opinion that in general German-Polish relations had stood the test. During the Czech crisis it had been shown that the German-Polish agreement was founded on a sound basis. Foreign Minister Beck believed that the straightforward Polish policy had been useful for Germany in winning the Sudeten area, and had made an important contribution toward a smoother solution of this question in the German sense. During these critical days the Polish Government had ignored all the siren songs which had been emitted from a certain quarter."³ Ribbentrop here interrupted Lipski and said that in his opinion, also, the German-Polish "agreement had proved itself to be invulnerable." The Foreign Minister added that through the Führer's action against Czechoslovakia Poland had satisfied her frontier wishes. Lipski then carried on to prove the importance of Danzig to Poland: "For centuries Danzig had been a free city, and had always served as Poland's outlet at the mouth of the Vistula, that is, the mouth of a purely Polish river; and therefore Danzig had also had a symbolic significance for Poland. The first partition of Poland at the time of Frederick the Great had begun with the severing of Danzig's natural connection with Poland. One must therefore understand that Poland was particularly sensitive in the Danzig question, for the Polish outlet to the sea was decisive for Poland's future. With the development of shipping and trade Gdynia would not be sufficient for Polish commerce. The customs union between Danzig and Poland was therefore of vital interest for Poland. For domestic political reasons also, Foreign Minister Beck could not agree to a union of Danzig with the Reich. If the Danzig question were opened, German-Polish relations would be profoundly and seriously endangered." "Foreign Minister Beck had now considered how all points of friction which might arise between Germany and Poland because of Danzig could be eliminated once and for all. He had thought that the League of Nations Statute for Danzig might be replaced by a German-Polish treaty in which all questions pertaining to Danzig would be dealt with. As a basis for this treaty Beck thought that one might fully recognize Danzig as a purely German city with all the rights resulting therefrom. On the other hand, however, Poland and the Polish minority should likewise be guaranteed all economic rights; thus Danzig's character as a free city and the customs union with Poland would be maintained. Since the National Socialist seizure of power the position of the Polish Government in the question of Danzig had become constantly more difficult. From month to month, even from day to day, the Polish Government had yielded to Danzig's demands. Poland had done nothing to counter the development of National Socialism in Danzig. However, Marshal Piłsudski had always stated that the treatment of the Danzig question was the measuring rod of German-Polish friendship, and remained decisive for German-Polish relations."

Ribbentrop told Lipski that he regretted the position taken by M. Beck and expressed surprise that "such a solution as the Führer had in mind could endanger German-Polish relations." "The suggestion for a long-term solution of the German-Polish problem by which Danzig would go to Germany might well result in domestic political difficulties for M. Beck, but on the other hand it should not be forgotten," Ribbentrop added, "that the Führer would not find it easy either to justify to the German people a guarantee of the Polish Corridor." The Foreign Minister concluded the conversation, stating that he had wanted "to create something permanent" in German-Polish relations and "bring about real stability," though that "could naturally not be done in a day." Ribbentrop also hoped that M. Beck would think about the German suggestions "at his leisure" and would "come to regard them in a positive light after all."

On January 5, 1939, Hitler received Beck at Berchtesgaden and took the initiative in discussing German-Polish relations in general, and Danzig in particular. Also present at this meeting were Ribbentrop, Moltke, Lipski and Lubinski. The Reich Chancellor stated that

> there had not been the slightest change in Germany's relations with Poland as based on the non-aggression declaration of 1934. Germany would under all circumstances be interested in maintaining a strong nationalist Poland, quite irrespective of developments in Russia. Regardless of whether Russia was bolshevist or czarist, or something else, Germany's attitude towards that country would always be one of the greatest caution and for that reason she was decidedly interested in seeing Poland's position preserved. Purely from the military point of view the existence of a strong Polish Army meant a considerable easing of Germany's position; the divisions which Poland stationed at the Russian frontier saved Germany just so much additional military expenditure.[4]

The Führer said that he wanted to "arrive at a definitive settlement" with Poland. In his opinion, he said, it was necessary to bring the city of Danzig into the German political community in "accordance with the will of its population." Naturally the Polish economic interests would be "fully protected." This was also in the interest of Danzig, "for Danzig could not live economically without Poland, either," and so the Führer said he was "thinking of a formula by which Danzig would come into the German community politically but remain with Poland economically." "Danzig is German," the Chancellor emphasized, "will always remain German, and will sooner or later become part of Germany." Hitler, however, assured Beck that no *fait accompli* would be "engineered in Danzig." The Führer confessed that the Corridor "was a difficult psychological problem for Germany" but it was, the Chancellor pointed out, "completely absurd to want to deprive Poland of her outlet to the sea": "If Poland were bottled up in this manner, she might, in view of the tension that would thereby arise be likened to a loaded revolver whose trigger might be pulled at any time. Thus, the necessity for Poland to have access to the sea definitely had to be recognized. In the same way, however, having a connection with East Prussia was a necessity for Germany; here too, by using entirely new methods of solution one could perhaps do justice to the interests of both." It was not easy for him, Hitler added, to guarantee the Corridor. He would be widely criticized, but as a "realistic statesman," he believed, he said, that "such a solution was the best": "When Germany had once given such a guarantee as little would be heard about the Polish Corridor as was being said today about the South Tyrol or Alsace-Lorraine."

The Polish Foreign Minister thanked the Chancellor for his "comprehensive exposition" of Germany's policy and assured the Chancellor that Poland would "absolutely adhere to the attitude she had adopted vis-à-vis Germany heretofore." Concerning Russia, Beck made it clear that Poland was trying to find an acceptable *modus vivendi* [arrangement for peaceful coexistence] with that country and that Poland had no intention of joining in a Pact with or against her. The Danzig question, Beck said, seemed "extremely difficult" to him. He had to consider public opinion in Poland, though during his 7-year tenure of office he had, Beck informed Hitler, never paid any attention to the "coffee-house opposition."

Both Hitler and Beck expressed their interest in Ukraine. But such problems were regarded as secondary to the German-Polish understanding.

Beck met Ribbentrop on January 6 and expressed his great concern over the reference made to Danzig by the Reich Chancellor.[5] The Polish Foreign Minister warned Ribbentrop that Danzig could be very disturbing and dangerous to German-Polish relations. Beck referred to two possibilities which would require Germany and Poland to take a stand on the following:

1. The League of Nations might disinterest itself in the Danzig question and withdraw its High Commissioner. Germany and Poland would then have to deal with the question themselves.
2. Any *faits accomplis* [situations already established] would force Poland to take a stand.

In answer to this Ribbentrop repeated his previous statements that it was his country's "profound desire" to establish a "definitive, comprehensive and generous consolidation of mutual relations" with Poland. In order to achieve that, Ribbentrop said, he could not see any solution other than the reincorporation of Danzig by Germany. Mentioning Ukraine, the Reich Foreign Minister told Beck that Germany had no direct interest in Polish Ukraine. German interest lay in the Soviet-Russian Ukraine only to the extent that Germany could inflict damage on Russia, just as she did on Germany. The two Foreign Ministers parted with the hope that they would turn over in their minds, the "whole problem of a possible treaty between Poland and Germany and leave to Lipski and Moltke to carry on the negotiations."

THE CRITICAL PERIOD OF MARCH–MAY 1939

Beck, after his meeting with Hitler on January 5, recorded that he was pessimistic about reaching an agreement with the German Government on Danzig.[6]

If Beck had any suspicions, they were confirmed when, on March 16, Germany granted protection to Slovakia. Moltke reported that Beck watched the Protection with "great interest." The Polish Foreign Minister wished to know the significance of this promise. Beck told Moltke that he was unable to understand this situation,[7] as Poland had unofficially signified her readiness to guarantee the frontiers,[8] and as there was no sign of a threat of an attack from Hungary, Moltke, in his despatches to Berlin, wrote that the announcement of this Protection had caused considerable uneasiness in the Polish Capital and given rise to anti-German demonstrations. The German Ambassador advised the Foreign Ministry in Berlin that Beck should be "supplied with information calculated to lessen as far as possible fears of a far-reaching infringement of Slovak independence and the danger of military pressure on Poland from Slovakia."[9]

Ribbentrop invited Lipski to call on him on March 21 and referred to the appeal that the "independent" Slovak Government had sent to Germany for protection. This Protection, Ribbentrop assured Lipski, was not directed against Poland. The Reich Foreign Minister also hinted that the question could be made a "subject of joint discussions if German-Polish relations in general developed satisfactorily."[10] Lipski protested that the Protection was a blow against Poland. Linguistically, the Ambassador said, Slovaks were related to Poles, and history played a part in determining Polish interests in this area. Thereupon, Ribbentrop complained against the "gradual stiffening" of German-Polish relations. He drew Lipski's attention to the incidents in Danzig provoked by the Polish students and to the anti-German press attacks in Poland. Hitherto Ribbentrop had, the Foreign Minister told Lipski, restrained the German press, but it was getting more and more difficult for him to hold the press back: Once the press attacks were answered there would be nothing left of German-Polish relations. The Führer wanted to live in understanding with Poland, but the Chancellor was, so Ribbentrop thought, "becoming increasingly amazed at Poland's attitude." Lipski "must admit," Ribbentrop remarked, that "Germany was not without her share in the creation and present existence of Poland. If at Brest Litovsk, for example, Germany had pursued a different policy with Russia, there would be no Poland today." "The basis on which German-Polish understanding could rest" the Foreign Minister added, "would only be provided by German and Polish nationalists. Poland must realize clearly that she could not take a middle course. Either Poland would remain a national State, working for a reasonable relationship with Germany and her Führer, or one day there would arise a Marxist Polish Government which would then be absorbed by Bolshevist Russia." Germany, Ribbentrop said, "most honestly desired that Poland should retain a strong National Government, as represented by Marshal Piłsudski's group of Colonels." "The Corridor settlement," the Foreign Minister went on to tell Lipski, "was generally felt to be the heaviest burden of the Versailles Treaty for Germany." No previous Government had been in a position to renounce German revisionist claims without being swept away by the Reichstag within forty-eight hours.

The Führer had other ideas about the problem of the Corridor. He recognized the justification of the Polish claim to free access to the sea. He was the only German Statesman who could pronounce a final renunciation of the Corridor. The condition for this, however, was the return of the purely German Danzig to the Reich as well as the establishment of extra-territorial rail and road connections between the Reich and East Prussia. Only this would remove the thorn in the flesh which the existence of the Corridor represented for the German people. If Polish statesmen would calmly take into account the real facts, a solution could be found on the following basis: "The return of Danzig to the Reich, extra-territorial rail and road connections between East Prussia and the Reich and, in return, a German guarantee for the Corridor. I could well imagine that in such circumstances it would be possible to deal with the Slovak question to the satisfaction of all." Lipski was also told that Germany was prepared to "regard the Ukrainian question from a purely Polish angle." The Polish Ambassador promised to inform Beck of the German proposals and to report on them immediately.

Lipski delivered his Government's instructions to the Reich Foreign Minister on March 26. The important suggestions in these proposals were:

1. The Polish Government "ascribe full importance to the maintenance of good neighbourly relations" with the German Government.
2. The Polish Government "have given clear proof of this attitude by being one of the first foreign Governments to initiate friendly relations with the German Reich already in 1933 and to enter into negotiations which led to the conclusion of the Polish-German Declaration of January 26, 1934."
3. Friendly attitude adopted by Poland towards the National Socialist Senate in Danzig.
4. It is well known that in the autumn of 1938, Poland's resolute attitude contributed in considerable degree to the avoidance of an armed conflict in connection with the accomplishment of the German demands.
5. The Polish Government had no interest in creating difficulties in traffic between East Prussia and the Reich, but any concession could "only be granted on the Polish side within the limits of Polish sovereignty—therefore there can be no question of extra territorial status for the ways of communication. While making this reservation, the Polish Government intend to meet German wishes very liberally." "This being their attitude, the Polish Government are prepared jointly with the German Government to study means of further simplifying and facilitating rail and road traffic between East Prussia and the rest of the Reich so that German travellers may be saved inconvenience when using these ways of communication. Technical experts could begin working out proposals for realizing this aim."

6. Concerning the Danzig problem, the Polish Government said: "As appeared from the previous Polish-German conversations, there existed no difference of opinion on the basic approach, namely that the Polish Government do not aim at hindering the German population of the Free City in their own way of life, that on the other hand the German Government respect Polish rights as well as the economic, maritime and transport interests, and the rights of the Polish population in the Free City. As these two questions are both fundamental, the Polish Government believe that it should be possible to find a solution based on a joint Polish-German guarantee for the Free City of Danzig. This guarantee would, on the other hand, satisfy the free development of the German national community and its political way of life, and on the other hand, would safeguard Polish rights and interests. Polish interests, moreover, coincide with the economic interests of the population of the Free City, as for centuries the prosperity of the latter has depended on Polish overseas trade.[11]

It was the first time that the Polish Government came out so outspokenly against surrendering their sovereignty over the Corridor and their rights in Danzig. Poland was prepared, as Lipski pointed out, to "find a solution based on a joint Polish-German guarantee of the Free City of Danzig," but the Polish Government made it clear that Poland was not considering an outright annexation of the Free City by Germany.

The Reich Foreign Minister told Lipski that in Ribbentrop's opinion Polish proposals would be regarded as unsatisfactory by the Führer and the Foreign Minister did not think that they would form a basis for the German-Polish solution. Only "the definite reincorporation of Danzig," Ribbentrop stressed, "an extra-territorial link with East Prussia, and a 25 year non-aggression treaty with frontier guarantees, and co-operation in the Slovak question could, in the German view, lead to a final settlement." At this conversation the Reich Foreign Minister also took the opportunity to discuss the recent Polish troop movement.[12]

Ribbentrop warned the Polish Ambassador against "possible consequences" of Polish troop concentration: If matters went so far, a "serious situation might soon arise." Ribbentrop also made it clear that a "violation of the sovereignty of Danzig territory by Polish troops would be regarded by Germany in the same way as a violation of the Reich frontiers." Lipski denied that Poland had any military intentions towards Danzig. Whatever troop movements Poland had undertaken were, Lipski assured Ribbentrop, only precautionary measures.

Moltke, on March 29, lodged another protest with the Polish Foreign Minister in Warsaw.[13] The Polish mobilization, the German Ambassador said to Beck, was "entirely unjustified" and a "very dubious step to take." The warlike atmosphere created by irresponsible press had given rise to a situation with "very dangerous possibilities." Beck justified the mobilization measures, stating that "the claim made precisely at this moment about Danzig, after the events in Czechoslovakia and Memel had had to be interpreted by Poland as a danger signal. There was no cause for anxiety that difficulties might arise in consequence of the measures."[14] Beck then referred to the German warning given by Ribbentrop to Lipski on March 26, that a Polish coup against Danzig would signify a *casus belli* [act to justify war] for Germany. The Polish Foreign Minister now warned Moltke that Beck was forced to state that, if an attempt were made by Germany or by the Danzig Senate to alter the existing status of Danzig, Poland would regard this as a *casus belli*. Beck regretted, he told Moltke, the exacerbation in German-Polish relations, and hoped to find a solution satisfactory to both sides.

The Polish warning of March 29 and the declaration[15] of the British Prime Minister on March 31 sharply changed German policy towards Poland. The Polish Government, Ribbentrop thought, had failed to see reason. He ordered a tougher line and for the Polish press attacks to be "thoroughly" answered in the German press. The Reich Foreign Minister rejected[16] the Polish "evasive answer" to the "generous proposals" made by Germany as a basis for settlement of the Danzig question. The German Embassy in Warsaw was told that the German offer to Poland was not to be repeated.[17] If Poland did not understand the significance of the German offer, the Germans could not, so they thought, help that. "The future would show," wrote Weizsäcker, "whether Poland had been well advised."[18] The German Ambassador in Warsaw was informed that the proposals put forward by the Polish Government had been rejected by the German Foreign Minister as a basis for negotiations, and that the Ambassador should not enter "into any further material discussions on the German offer and the Polish counter offer." "We must prevent Poland," Weizsäcker advised Moltke, "from throwing the ball back to us and then manoeuvring us into the position of appearing to have let a Polish offer go unheeded."[19]

The Polish Government, on April 6, communicated their views to the German Embassy in Warsaw,[20] explaining why they had welcomed the British declaration of March 31: It was the result of Germany's pressure on Poland. Although such a method could never be successfully used against the Polish Government, it created a state of anxiety in Poland. By taking an intransigent stand on Danzig, the Polish Government had saved German-Polish relations, for if the Polish Foreign Minister compromised with the German view-point, Beck would have been forced to resign. Such a development would have given rise to anti-German policy in Poland and pushed the country into an alliance with the Soviet Union. The Embassy was further informed that the

Polish Government still desired to come to an understanding with Germany, though under condition that no pressure was employed and that the independence of the two countries was maintained.

Hitler wrote down in his Directive of April 11, that German relations with Poland "continue to be based on the principles of avoiding any disturbances" but should Poland "however, change her policy towards Germany, which so far has been based on the same principles as our own, and adopt a threatening attitude towards Germany, a final settlement might become necessary in spite of the Treaty in force with Poland."[21] His aim was, he wrote, to isolate Poland and to crush her. The object of the *Wehrmacht*[Armed Forces], Hitler outlined in his Directive, would be to destroy the Polish Armed Forces: And this could be attained only by a sudden surprise attack. General mobilization was not to be ordered before the day of attack and "at the latest possible moment." The war would be limited to Poland only, and a conflict with the Western opponents avoided as far as possible. Hitler also hoped that the "development of increasing internal crisis in France and resulting British restraint might produce such a situation in the distant future."

Whereas preparations for war against Poland were still in the making, the German Chancellor proposed to show his good faith, as he said, in his speech of April 28, by offering to negotiate with Poland. In this speech to the Reichstag, Hitler condemned the Anglo-Polish Mutual Guarantee as obligations contradictory to the German-Polish Agreement of 1934, and declared that there was still hope for a peaceful solution. He said that he looked upon the 1934 Pact with Poland "as having been unilaterally infringed by Poland and thereby no longer in existence," but was ready to be reasonable and negotiate with the Polish Government. Hitler repeated the proposals his Foreign Minister had previously submitted to Lipski. The Führer regretted Poland's "incomprehensible attitude" of rejecting his offer. Posterity, the Chancellor said, would "one day decide whether it was really right to refuse this suggestion made this once" by him.[22]

The Polish Foreign Minister answered Hitler, in his speech to the Sejm on May 5.[23] Beck denied that the Anglo-Polish Mutual Guarantee in any way conflicted with the German-Polish Pact of 1934. An understanding with Great Britain, Beck said, was in no way an attempt to encircle Germany. Beck defended his policy, stating that he had been forced to conclude the London agreement,[24] by Polish public opinion, which had grown overwhelmingly anti-German. The Polish Foreign Minister asserted that it was his intention to restore the balance vis-à-vis the Reich, and to prevent the presentation of *faits accomplis* by other Powers. The Polish Government could not, Beck declared,

> accept such an interpretation of the Declaration of 1934 as would be equivalent to a renunciation of the right to conclude political agreements with third States

and, consequently almost a renunciation of independence in foreign policy. The policy of the German Reich in recent years has clearly indicated that the German Government have not drawn conclusions of this sort from the Declaration as far as they themselves were concerned. The undertakings publicly accepted by the Reich towards Italy and the German-Slovak Agreement of March, 1939 are clear indications of such an interpretation by the German Government of the Declaration of 1934. The Polish Government must here recall that in their relations with other States they give and require full reciprocity as being the only possible foundation of normal relations between States.[25]

"The Polish Government reject as completely without foundation all accusations regarding the alleged incompatibility of the Anglo-Polish Mutual Guarantee of April 1939 with the Polish-German Declaration of 1934. This guarantee has a purely defensive character and in no way threatens the German Reich, in the same way as the Polish-French alliance, whose compatibility with the Declaration of 1934 has been recognized by the German Reich." Should, however, Germany attack Poland, Beck made it clear, the Polish-British alliance would come into operation. The Polish Foreign Minister then appealed to Hitler, that the Polish Government wanted to live in peace with Germany and proposed the following as a basis for negotiations:

1. A joint Polish-German guarantee of the Free City of Danzig, the "existence of which was to be based on complete freedom of the local population in internal affairs and on the assurance of respect for Polish rights and interests."
2. Poland would provide liberal transit facilities but would not "give up her sovereignty over the belt of territory through which the transit route would run."

The German Government found nothing new or substantial in the Polish Memorandum,[26] nor did they think that Beck's speech to the Sejm was any contribution towards reaching an understanding with Germany. Weizsäcker found no "answering echo" in Beck's speech to the Führer's offer of April 28, "despite its accommodating and peaceable tone." Whatever the Polish Foreign Minister said, it was, the Germans concluded, "a relatively insignificant pronouncement by a weak Government."[27]

NOTES

1. Memorandum by Hewel, October 24, 1938, in German Foreign Ministry, *Documents on German Foreign Policy, 1918–1945*, Series D, Volume 5, *Poland, the*

Balkans, Latin America, the Smaller Powers, June 1937–March 1939 (London: H. M. Stationery Office, 1953), No. 81.

2. Republic of Poland, *Official Documents Concerning Polish-German and Polish-Soviet Relations, 1933–1939* (*Polish White Book*) (London: Ministry for Foreign Affairs for the Republic of Poland, 1939), No. 45 (hereafter cited as "Polish White Book").

3. Memorandum by Ribbentrop, November 19, 1938, German Foreign Ministry, *German Foreign Policy*, Series D, Volume 5, No. 101.

4. Memorandum by Schmidt, January 5, 1939, in German Foreign Ministry, *German Foreign Policy*, Series D, Volume 5, No. 119.

5. Memorandum by Ribbentrop, January 6, 1939, in German Foreign Ministry, *German Foreign Policy*, Series D, Volume 5, No. 120.

6. Republic of Poland, "Polish White Book," No. 49.

7. March 17, 1939, in German Foreign Ministry, *Documents on German Foreign Policy, 1918–1945*, Series D, Volume 6, *The Last Months of Peace, March–August 1939*, (London: H. M. Stationery Office, 1956), No. 12.

8. On March 16, Beck had expressed satisfaction with independent Slovakia, and informed Moltke that Poland had no designs in Slovakia. Noted in German Foreign Ministry, *German Foreign Policy*, Series D, Volume 6, No. 12.

9. German Foreign Ministry, *German Foreign Policy*, Series D, Volume 6, No. 12.

10. Memorandum by Ribbentrop, March 21, 1939, in German Foreign Ministry, *German Foreign Policy*, Series D, Volume 6, No. 16.

11. German Foreign Ministry, *German Foreign Policy*, Series D, Volume 6, No. 101, Enclosure I; Republic of Poland, "Polish White Book," No. 62.

12. Before the Polish Government submitted their proposals on March 26, Germany had scored another victory. Memel was reincorporated in the German Reich on March 22, and on March 23, Hitler landed in the city. Poland, fearing a coup in Danzig, mobilized her forces along the Polish-Danzig border. The German Consul General in Danzig, von Jansen, reported on March 24 that "measures of a purely defensive nature" had been taken by Poland in the northern part of the Corridor (German Foreign Ministry, *German Foreign Policy*, Series D, Volume 6, No. 85). Admiral Canaris gave the following information about Polish mobilization measures: (1) Some 4,000 Polish troops are concentrated at Gdynia; (2) The troops of a garrison previously stationed in the southern part of the Corridor have been transferred to the immediate vicinity of the Danzig frontier; and (3) Poland has mobilized three age-groups.

"All these measures concern only the northern part of Poland; in the other districts of the country there is nothing to report militarily. General Keitel does not believe in any aggressive intentions on the part of the Poles, neither, therefore, does he believe that Poland wishes rather to forestall us by a military occupation of Danzig, but attributes these measures to the generally noticeable nervousness of the Poles. In the General Staff on the other hand, the tendency is to take a somewhat more serious view of the situation" (Memorandum by Bismarck, March 25, 1939, in German Foreign Ministry, *German Foreign Policy*, Series D, Volume 6, No. 90). On March 25, Weizsäcker advised Ribbentrop that Poland should be warned not to bring the situation to a climax (German Foreign Ministry, *German Foreign Policy*, Series D, Volume 6, No. 90, n. 1).

13. German Foreign Ministry, *German Foreign Policy*, Series D, Volume 6, No. 118.

14. German Foreign Ministry, *German Foreign Policy*, Series D, Volume 6.

15. On March 31, Mr. Chamberlain made the following declaration in the House of Commons:

As I said this morning, His Majesty's Government have no official confirmation of the rumours of any projected attack on Poland and they must not therefore be taken as accepting them as true. I am glad to take this opportunity of stating again the general policy of His Majesty's Government. They have constantly advocated the adjustment, by way of free negotiation between the parties concerned, of any differences that may arise between them. They consider that this is the natural and proper course where differences exist. In their opinion there should be no question incapable of solution by peaceful means and they would see no justification for the substitution of force or threats of force for the method of negotiation. As the House is aware, certain consultations are now proceeding with other Governments. In order to make perfectly clear the position of His Majesty's Government in the meantime before those consultations are concluded, I now have to inform the House that during that period, in the event of any action which clearly threatened Polish independence, and which the Polish Government accordingly considered it vital to resist with their national forces, His Majesty's Government would feel themselves bound at once to lend the Polish Government all support in their power. They have given the Polish Government an assurance to this effect" (Great Britain, *House of Commons Parliamentary Debates*, March 31, 1939, Volume 3e45, col. 2415, https://www.parliament.uk/business/publications/hansard/commons/ [accessed October 21, 2019]).

The German Chargé d'Affaires in London, Herr Kordt, made the following comments on the British declaration:

> It is particularly significant that British assistance will become effective only when it is established, first, that German action clearly threatens Polish independence (in the judgment of Britain) and, secondly, that the Polish Government "accordingly" consider it vital to counter German action by military assistance. (1) The pledge of assistance on the fulfilment of both conditions operates only for the period up to the conclusion of the negotiations still in progress; (2) The first part of the statement leaves the settlement of all controversial points, including colonial questions, open to negotiation; (3) The second part of the statement leaves it doubtful, to say the least, whether military action against Danzig constitutes a *casus belli* for the British Government" (German Foreign Ministry, *German Foreign Policy*, Series D, Volume 6, No. 137).

Herr Kordt, in his observations to the Foreign Ministry, seems to have overlooked the statement that the British Government left it to the Poles to decide what they considered to be the national threat and His Majesty's Government would then "feel themselves bound at once to lend the Polish Government all support in their power." It was not then, as the Chargé d'Affaires put it, that Great Britain would come to the assistance of Poland only when German action, "in the judgment of Britain" clearly threatened Polish independence. Kordt was also wrong in expressing his doubt: "whether military action against Danzig constitutes a *casus belli* for the British Government." Perhaps he was not aware of the Polish démarche of March 29, in which Poland made it clear to the German Government that any military measures undertaken by Germany against Danzig would constitute a *casus belli* for Poland. Naturally then, what constituted a *casus belli* for the Polish Government was automatically a *casus belli* for Great Britain.

16. Ribbentrop to Lipski, March 27, 1939, in German Foreign Ministry, *German Foreign Policy*, Series D, Volume 6, No. 108. "A strong note, on the instructions of the Führer, was drafted to be sent to Moltke on March 23. The Note was not, on the advice of the Führer, sent to Moltke. Although the substance of this draft did not differ greatly from the Lipski-Ribbentrop conversation of March 21, the Note was, Weizsäcker explained to Moltke, "more sharply worded." This would have, Weizsäcker thought, "presented the Poles with the option: friend or foe"—an option which the German Foreign Ministry presumably wanted to avoid" (Weizsäcker to Moltke, March 24, 1939, in German Foreign Ministry, *German Foreign Policy*, Series D, Volume 6, No. 88). Outlining the German proposals for Danzig and the Corridor and the German policy towards Slovakia this note also read:

In weighing up correctly all these points of view it would be completely erroneous to say that by the reincorporation of Danzig into the Reich, Poland was exchanging something really concrete for merely abstract or vague assurances. The Polish Government could certainly be in no doubt that, however the separate politics of both Governments developed, Danzig could in no case be permanently prevented from union with the Reich. Poland should therefore not commit the serious mistake of clinging obstinately to a position which in the long run must prove untenable. Now that we had already repeatedly offered the Polish Government a solution on the above-mentioned basis, without receiving any positive response, we naturally could not repeat this offer *ad infinitum* [in perpetuity]. Indeed, if the Polish Government still adopt a purely passive or evasive attitude, the Führer is resolved to withdraw his offer once and for all, as we could only interpret such an attitude on the part of Poland as a direct rejection of our intentions and as an attitude directed in principle against the Third Reich. (German Foreign Ministry, *German Foreign Policy*, Series D, Volume 6, No. 73)

"In his Directive to the C-in-C of the Army, Hitler on March 25, (concerning Danzig) declared that he "*does not* wish to solve the Danzig problem by force however," nor "wish to drive Poland into the arms of Britain by this." "A possible military occupation of Danzig could be contemplated *only* if L(ipski) gave an indication that the Polish Government could not justify voluntary cession of Danzig to their own people and that a *fait accompli* would make a solution easier to them" (italics in original). "The cancellation of the strong Note and the Military Directive of March 25 justify, to a certain extent, that Hitler was careful, at this stage, not to cause any serious offence to the Polish Foreign Ministry and hoped that Poland would concede to the German demands peacefully" (German Foreign Ministry, *German Foreign Policy*, Series D, Volume 6, No. 99).

17. Weizsäcker to Moltke, April 5, 1939, in German Foreign Ministry, *German Foreign Policy*, Series D, Volume 6, No. 159.
18. German Foreign Ministry, *German Foreign Policy*, Series D, Volume 6.
19. German Foreign Ministry, *German Foreign Policy*, Series D, Volume 6.
20. Count Lubienski, *Chef de Cabinet* to the Polish Foreign Minister, had invited a member of the German Embassy, in order to communicate the views of the Polish Government (Moltke to the Foreign Ministry, April 6, 1939, in German Foreign Ministry, *German Foreign Policy*, Series D, Volume 6, No. 167).
21. Directive by the Führer, April 11, 1939, in German Foreign Ministry, *German Foreign Policy*, Series D, Volume 6, No. 185. The military preparations of "Operation White" were to be made in such a way that the actual operations could be carried out at any time as from September 1, 1939 (Directive by the Chief of the High Command of *Wehrmacht*, Keitel, April 3, 1939, in German Foreign Ministry, *German Foreign Policy*, Series D, Volume 6, No. 149).
22. Adolf Hitler, *The Speeches of Adolf Hitler, April 1922–August 1939*, ed. Norman H. Baynes (London: Oxford University Press, 1942). vol. 2, 1629–32. A note on similar terms was sent by the German Government to the Polish Government on April 27, 1939, in German Foreign Ministry, *German Foreign Policy*, Series D, Volume 6, No. 276.
23. Great Britain, "Speech Made by M. Beck, the Polish Minister for Foreign Affairs in Parliament on May 5, 1939," in *The British War Bluebook*, cmd. 6106, No. 15, https://avalon.law.yale.edu/wwii/blbk15.asp (accessed October 21, 2019). See also Republic of Poland, "Polish White Book," No. 77.
24. Great Britain, "Anglo-Polish Communiqué Issued on April 6, 1939," in *The British War Bluebook*, No. 18, https://avalon.law.yale.edu/wwii/blbk18.asp (accessed October 21, 2019).; Republic of Poland, "Polish White Book," No. 77.
25. Great Britain, "Anglo-Polish Communiqué Issued on April 6, 1939"; Republic of Poland, "Polish White Book," No. 77.
26. The Polish Government submitted on May 5, 1939, a Memorandum to the German Government which coincided with Beck's speech to the Sejm (German Foreign Ministry, *German Foreign Policy*, Series D, Volume 6, No. 334).
27. Circular of the State Secretary, May 6, 1939, in German Foreign Ministry, *German Foreign Policy*, Series D, Volume 6, No. 335.

Chapter 4

The Polish Ultimatum to the Danzig Senate

The ever existing possibility that the Danzig Senate might face Poland with a *fait accompli* left the Polish Government in a very restless state. Poland expressed anxiety over the creation of a "psychosis" in Danzig, the purpose of which was, so the Poles thought, to convince the population of Danzig that the city would be in the near future annexed to the German Reich. In this context the Polish Government warned the Danzig Senate that such a procedure would be in contradiction to the declaration made by the Führer, the declaration by the Senate and other existing treaties and agreements. Warsaw made it known in Danzig that Poland could protest juridically—on the basis of International Law—and also take political and economic measures.[1]

Poland had two national questions, the Polish diplomatic representative in Danzig, Chodacki, told Greiser, President of the Danzig Senate: The army and the sea. Poles would, irrespective of their political affiliations, attack any one who attacked the army. Polish people were striving towards the open sea, which was part of the national question. Danzig was part of this national question. Any political action which interfered with this access to the sea would meet resistance from every Pole. The Polish Government, Chodacki added, was willing to recognize the German "element" and National Socialism in Danzig and agree to its internal policies so far as such measures did not infringe on Polish "desires and rights."

On November 15, 1938 an ordinance which barred Jews from the civil service was published by the Government of the Free City of Danzig[2] and another ordinance prohibiting marriages between Jews and Aryans was published on November 23.[3] The Danzig Senate was proposing to enact these laws. Such measures affected Polish Jews as well. The Polish Government thought that these laws were a clear violation of the original Danzig constitution which provided that there "was to be no discrimination against Polish nationals or against Danzig nationals of Polish origin and speech." The

League High Commissioner, Mr. Burckhardt, expressed his misgivings to the Senate President Greiser, whether it was expedient at that time to enact such laws.[4] Gauleiter Forster answered and justified the introduction of these laws on the grounds that they did not apply to Polish Jews in so far as there was hardly a Jew in the Danzig civil service. The Gauleiter also thought that "precautions had at long last to be taken in German Danzig too, to prevent Jews from violating German women and girls at will."[5]

The League High Commissioner protested to Ribbentrop.[6] The Foreign Minister advised the Gauleiter on January 13, 1939 not to undertake any new steps in Danzig until it would be decided "whether new measures shall be initiated in Danzig or whether such measures would be rendered superfluous by a general settlement with Poland."[7] Ribbentrop changed his attitude after the Polish Note of March 26 in which Poland had made it clear that she was not willing to compromise on the status of Danzig or the Corridor. Weizsäcker was directed to advise the Danzig Senate that they "had no cause to show the Polish Government a particularly accommodating attitude in the treatment of Danzig-Polish questions," but they were not to "provoke Poland in any way through Danzig."[8] In a conversation with Greiser, Ribbentrop told the Senate President (March 29) that Germany would adopt "attrition tactics" towards Poland in order to make the Polish Government "more disposed to the settlement aimed at" by Germany: While the German Government would continue to assert their demands on Poland, Danzig would adopt a "Sphinx-like" attitude towards Poland.[9]

Both the Danzig Senate and the Polish Government were very sensitive about their respective rights in Danzig. Thus the relations between the two were never what one can call stable. The unfortunate incident on the night of May 20–21 only made them worse. That night on the Polish–Danzig border, in Danzig territory near Kalthof, a national of the Danzig Free State was shot dead from the motor car of the Polish Diplomatic Mission in Danzig. The occupant of the car, among others was, as the Danzig Senate reported, the Counsellor of the Polish Legation in Danzig, M. Perkowski. Greiser sent a Note of Protest to the Polish Diplomatic representative in Danzig.[10] Chodacki denied the accusation that the incident was caused deliberately. Poland claimed that the incident had occurred in self-defence.[11] Greiser, on June 3, sent another note to Chodacki complaining against the increase in the number of Polish customs inspectors.[12] Greiser wrote that the Danzig population felt themselves constantly offended by the behaviour of the Polish customs officers while performing their duty and by their behaviour in their private lives. The Senate President therefore insisted that the Polish officials must perform their duties inside and not outside their office buildings. He had, Greiser wrote, also forbidden the Danzig Customs Officials to take instructions from the Polish Customs Officials. Chodacki was further informed that

Greiser had left it to the discretion of the Finance Department of the Senate to administer the oath of loyalty to the National Socialist "leadership" to the Customs Officials, if they regarded it as desirable. Chodacki, on June 12, rejecting the complaints made against the conduct of the Polish Officers, wrote to Greiser that Poland would not permit restrictions on the rights of the Polish Customs Officers and if the Danzig Customs Officials were sworn in, the Polish Government would consider increasing the number of Customs Officers, since the Danzig Customs Officials "can then be relied upon still less than hitherto to respect the Polish Customs regulations and to apply them properly."[13]

The German Ambassador reported from Warsaw that such development as had recently taken place in Danzig, had been interpreted in Poland as a sign that Germany was determined to solve the Danzig question by force if necessary. Moltke also gathered that Poland felt that her rights had been violated and that counteraction would be necessary. The Ambassador warned Berlin that the country was determined to fight if she was denied her treaty rights.[14]

On July 19, the Polish Government sent another protest, to the Senate President; this time against the insulting behaviour of the Danzig Customs Inspectors towards the Polish officials.[15] The Polish note demanded an "unequivocal" statement from the Senate of the Free City to guarantee the condition under which the Polish Inspectors could carry out their duties. Failing to obtain such a guarantee, the Polish Government would, the note said, consider economic measures against Danzig. The Senate of the Free City, in their Note of July 29, accused the Polish Customs Inspectors of espionage and defended their "special supervisory measures" on those grounds.[16] The Danzig Note asserted that any economic measures taken by the Polish Government against the Free City would compel the Senate to apply economic reprisals.

The Danzig Senate were preparing to issue instructions,[17] that the Danzig State's Customs Authority should no longer recognize the "so called Polish frontier guards" as Customs Inspectors as from August 6. The Polish Representative, Chodacki, found out about this and addressed to the Senate President a strong protest, tantamount to an ultimatum, Chodacki wrote,

> I have learned, that the local Danzig Custom Authorities at the frontier posts between the Free City of Danzig and East Prussia have approached the Polish Customs Inspectors with a statement, unexampled of its kind, that the Danzig administrative authorities intend, from 7 a.m. on August 6, to resist a certain section of the Polish Inspectors in the performance of their control functions, which functions arise out of the rights of the Polish Government on the Customs frontier. I am convinced that this action of the local authorities is either due to a misunderstanding or to a false interpretation of the instructions of the Senate of the Free City of Danzig.

I do not doubt that you, Mr. President of the Senate, have no doubts that such an infringement of the fundamental rights of Poland would under no pretext be tolerated by the Polish Government.

I await your answer assuring me that you have issued orders which cancel the action of your subordinates, at the latest by 6 p.m. on August 5.

In view of the fact that the above-mentioned action has taken place at a number of frontier posts, I am compelled to warn you, Mr. President of the Senate, that all Polish Customs Inspectors have received the order to carry out their duties in uniform and with arms on August 6, 1939, and the following days at all points on the frontier which they regard as necessary for control. All attempts to hamper them in the performance of their duties, all attacks or intervention by the police authorities will be regarded as acts of violence against officials of the Polish State during the performance of their duties.

Should the above-mentioned abuses take place the Polish Government will retaliate without delay against the Free City, and the responsibility for this will fall exclusively on the Senate of the Free City.

I hope to receive a satisfactory explanation by the time stated.[18]

The Senate, on August 5, "temporarily suspended" the execution of any such instructions. The matter was postponed until Gauleiter Forster received new instructions from the Führer.[19] President Greiser, in his Note of August 7, expressed astonishment at a "completely unauthenticated rumour" which had occasioned Chodacki to send a "short term ultimatum."[20] The Danzig Government, in this Note, protested very strongly against the Polish "unwarrantable threat, the consequences of which will fall upon the Polish Government."

The Polish ultimatum of August 5 to the Danzig Senate provoked Hitler's indignation. A repetition of such a note to Danzig, he said to the Hungarian Foreign Minister on August 8, would be "appropriately answered" by Germany.[21] The German people, the Chancellor said, were now more anti-Polish than they had been anti-Czech. Other observations Hitler made in his conversation with the Hungarian Foreign Minister were: Poland presented no problem to Germany: "The tension with Poland had brought him the fanatical 100 per cent support of the Army as well as that of the last remaining opposition, namely certain Prussian aristocratic families who had been unable to understand his previous accommodating attitude to Poland." The "mood of the German Army, which had been divided, was such that it would be a terrible disappointment for them if the Poles were, after all, to see reason at the last minute. The German people, who had not understood the policy of reconciliation hitherto adopted towards Poland, were of the same mind." He was "reckoning from the start with a war on two fronts, which, if it came, would be conducted with a lightening speed." The Polish army and the

Polish State would be totally destroyed. Germany had very strong defensive and offensive power; Britain did not scare him.

On August 9, Weizsäcker received the Polish Chargé d'Affaires in Berlin and told him that the Reich Government were surprised at the Polish Note of August 4 to the Danzig Senate.[22] The German Government were obliged to point out, Weizsäcker said, that a "repetition of such demands in the form of an ultimatum to the Free City of Danzig and threat of reprisals would lead to an aggravation of German-Polish relations, for the consequences of which responsibility would fall exclusively on the Polish Government and for which the Reich Government must now at this stage disclaim all responsibility." Weizsäcker further read out, that, should the Polish Government take economic measures against the Free City, the Senate would then have to explore "other possibilities for exports and, of course, also for imports."

The Polish Government, on August 10, communicated that they had noted with "extreme surprise" the German protest of August 9.[23] The Government of the Polish Republic, the Polish Note stated, could "in fact see no legal grounds to justify Germany's intervention in these relations": "That exchanges of views on the Danzig problem have been possible between the Polish Government and the Reich Government has been due solely to the goodwill of the Polish Government and did not derive from any obligation." The Polish Government, the Note read, were compelled to tell the Reich Government that they will "continue to react as hitherto to any attempt by the authorities of the Free City to impair the rights and interests which Poland enjoys in Danzig under the agreements and will do so by such means and measures as they alone may deem appropriate, and that they will regard any interventions by the Reich Government to the detriment of these rights and interests as an act of aggression."

The German Embassy in Warsaw was instructed by the Foreign Minister to "maintain a purely receptive attitude, and to confine itself exclusively to sending communications of an informatory character to Berlin."[24] The Embassy was also directed not to enter into any political negotiations or to have contact with any Polish authority. After the Polish reply of August 10, Weizsäcker advised the Embassy that their most urgent task was to "reproduce as extensively as possible opinions expressed in the Polish press which could be turned to political advantage" in the German press.[25] These reports should include, Weizsäcker asked: "all anti-German utterances," "war-mongering and aggressively annexationist opinions"; also such domestic events as "persecution of Germans," "oppression of Ukrainians," etc. etc.

The German Government instructed the German missions abroad not to initiate any conversation in their capitals on the German-Polish exchanges of Notes.[26] If, however, the Missions were questioned about such exchanges, the

Polish Communication of August 10 was to be shown as a "further proof of megalomania and the warmongering policy of the Polish rulers."

NOTES

1. Chodacki to Greiser, December 22, 1938, in German Foreign Ministry, *Documents on German Foreign Policy, 1918–1945*, Series D, Volume 5, *Poland, the Balkans, Latin America, the Smaller Powers, June 1937–March 1939* (London: H. M. Stationery Office, 1953), No. 116.

2. Beamtengesetz, *Gesetzblatt für die Freie Stadt Danzig*, in German Foreign Ministry, *German Foreign Policy*, Series D, Volume 5, No. 74.

3. *Gesetzblatt*, in German Foreign Ministry, *German Foreign Policy*, Series D, Volume 5, No. 77.

4. Memorandum by Schliep, October 20, 1938, in German Foreign Ministry, *German Foreign Policy*, Series D, Volume 5, No. 671; Minute by Boltcher, December 7, 1938, in German Foreign Ministry, *German Foreign Policy*, Series D, Volume 5, No. 674.

5. Forster to Burckhardt, December 13, 1938, in German Foreign Ministry, *German Foreign Policy*, Series D, Volume 5, No. 676.

6. Ribbentrop agreed with Burckhardt that such laws required legal sanction by a newly elected Danzig Assembly. Memorandum by Weizsäcker, December 19, 1938, in German Foreign Ministry, *German Foreign Policy*, Series D, Volume 5, No. 114.

7. Note by Hewel, January 13, 1939, in German Foreign Ministry, *German Foreign Policy*, Series D, Volume 5, No. 122.

8. Memorandum by Weizsäcker, March 29, 1939, in German Foreign Ministry, *Documents on German Foreign Policy, 1918–1945*, Series D, Volume 6, *The Last Months of Peace, March–August 1939* (London: H. M. Stationery Office, 1956), No. 124.

9. Schliep to Moltke, March 29, 1939, in German Foreign Ministry, *German Foreign Policy*, Series D, Volume 6, No. 126.

10. Memorandum by Bergmann, May 21, 1939, in German Foreign Ministry, *German Foreign Policy*, Series D, Volume 6, No. 417.

11. The Polish Diplomatic Representative in Danzig to the President of the Danzig Senate, May 21, 1939. Translation of the Text, in German Foreign Ministry, *German Foreign Policy*, Series D, Volume 6, No. 418.

12. Greiser to Chodacki, June 3, 1939, in German Foreign Ministry, *German Foreign Policy*, Series D, Volume 6, No. 471.

13. Janson to the Foreign Ministry, June 12, 1939, in German Foreign Ministry, *German Foreign Policy*, Series D, Volume 6, No. 515.

14. Moltke to the Foreign Ministry, July 6, 1939, in German Foreign Ministry, *German Foreign Policy*, Series D, Volume 6, No. 622.

15. Janson to the Foreign Ministry, July 22, 1939, in German Foreign Ministry, *German Foreign Policy*, Series D, Volume 6, No. 702.

16. Janson to the Foreign Ministry, July 31, 1939, in German Foreign Ministry, *German Foreign Policy*, Series D, Volume 6, No. 749.

17. Memorandum by Bergmann, August 5, 1939, in German Foreign Ministry, *German Foreign Policy*, Series D, Volume 6, No. 774.

18. Polish Representative Chodacki, August 4, 1939, in German Foreign Ministry, *German Foreign Policy*, Series D, Volume 6, No. 774, Enclosure.

19. Memorandum by Bergmann, August 5, 1939, in German Foreign Ministry, *German Foreign Policy*, Series D, Volume 6, No. 774.

20. Greiser to Chodacki, August 7, 1939, in *German Foreign Policy*, Series D, Volume 6, No. 780.

21. Memorandum by Erdmannsdorff, August 8, 1939, in German Foreign Ministry, *German Foreign Policy*, Series D, Volume 6, No. 784.

22. The text was telephoned to Weizsäcker by Ribbentrop on August 8, in German Foreign Ministry, *Documents on German Foreign Policy, 1918–1945*, Series D, Volume 7, *The Last Days of Peace, August 9–September 3, 1939* (London: H. M. Stationery Office, 1956), No. 5.

23. German Foreign Ministry, *German Foreign Policy*, Series D, Volume 7, No. 10.

24. Memorandum by Woermann, August 9, 1939, in German Foreign Ministry, *German Foreign Policy*, Series D, Volume 6, No. 2.

25. Weizsäcker to the Embassy in Poland, August 13, 1939, in German Foreign Ministry, *German Foreign Policy*, Series D, Volume 7, No. 46.

26. German Foreign Ministry, *German Foreign Policy*, Series D, Volume 7, No. 57.

Chapter 5

The Tug-of-War for the Soviet Alliance

After the intransigent Polish attitude towards Germany, and the British guarantee to Poland on April 6, both Germany and Great Britain realized that in order to pursue their respective foreign policies they would need the assistance of the Soviet Union. A brief description of the British and German attitudes vis-à-vis the Soviet Union is therefore necessary.

THE BRITISH EFFORTS TO SEEK AN ALLIANCE

Lord Halifax, on April 4, told Beck that he had no doubts that one day Great Britain and Poland might suddenly be in trouble together and it might then be important to Poland to "be able to use the Russian route for the supply of war material."[1] Halifax thought it appropriate to "get a maximum degree of collaboration from Soviet Russia."[2] The Foreign Secretary wrote to Seeds, the British Ambassador in Moscow, that he was reluctant to abandon his efforts to "secure some measure of co-operation from the Soviet Government."[3] The Foreign Office took the initiative and informed the Soviet Government that His Majesty's Government had noted with satisfaction the pronouncement[4] that the Soviet Union would be prepared to render support to nations who were the victims of aggression and who fought for their independence. This statement was thought by His Majesty's Government to be in complete accord with British foreign policy. Seeds was thus asked to enquire[5] if the Soviet Government would be willing to make a "positive declaration" on their "own initiative" that "in the event of any act of aggression against any European neighbour of the Soviet Union which was resisted by the country concerned the assistance of the Soviet Government would be available, if desired, and would be afforded in such a manner as would be found most convenient."

The Soviet Government responded quickly. They regarded, the Soviets said, the British enquiry and the French proposals[6] as acceptable in principle and desired to place relations between the three States on a "solid foundation." Litvinov put forward the Soviet proposals, claiming that they were an attempt to combine the British and the French proposals.[7] The most important parts of these proposals were: That Great Britain, France and the Soviet Union should conclude an agreement "by which they would oblige themselves to render mutually forthwith all manner of assistance," and that this agreement would further undertake to assist "Eastern European States situated between Baltic and Black seas and bordering on U.S.S.R. in case of aggression against these States."

His Majesty's Government, the Foreign Secretary on May 6 wrote to Seeds,[8] gave a careful and sympathetic consideration to the Soviet counter-proposals, and appreciated the readiness with which the Soviet Government had responded. The British Government regretted the delay in answering the Soviet Plan. Such delay as had occurred, Halifax wrote, had been "unavoidable not only because they have felt it right themselves to examine the Soviet Plan with all the care that so important a proposal deserves, but also because they have been in duty bound to communicate with other interested Governments before reaching their own conclusions." Halifax explained that the British Government could not accept proposals whereby the Soviet Union would be "bound automatically to render military assistance" to States "most immediately threatened."[9] The British Government proposed that "in the event of Great Britain and France being involved in hostilities" in fulfilment of the British and French obligations "to certain Eastern European countries" the "assistance of the Soviet Government would be immediately available, if desired, and would be afforded in such a manner and on such terms as might be agreed." This "formula," Halifax added, "does in fact, give the Soviet Government a reciprocal assurance of common action, since the declaration which we would suggest to be made by them only places them under a conditional obligation in a case where *ex hypothesi* [it is supposed] Great Britain and France are already engaged."

On May 11, *Izvestiya* [News] published an article[10] which the British Embassy in Moscow considered to represent the views of the Soviet Government. The article expressed the view that "co-operation presupposes reciprocity as its natural basis. Where there is no reciprocity there is no possibility of establishing real co-operation." The only way to "set up a barrier against aggression in Europe," the article read, would be to "create a united front of mutual assistance" between England, France and the U.S.S.R. and to extend the guarantee to other Powers in "Eastern and Central Europe which are under the menace of aggression."

Molotov, who replaced Litvinov on May 3, 1939, handed the reply of the Soviet Government to Seeds, on May 15.[11] The Soviet Government communicated that the British proposals could not serve as a "basis for organisation of a front of resistance against a further extension of aggression in Europe." This conclusion was based on several considerations. Briefly these were: "The British proposals do not contain the principle of reciprocity"; they do not "guarantee the U.S.S.R. in the event of a direct attack on the latter by aggressors"; and the "fact that north western frontier of U.S.S.R. remains uncovered may serve to provoke aggression in the direction of Soviet Union." The Soviet Note read that the Soviet Government

> consider there are at least three indispensable conditions for creation of an effective barrier by pacific States against a further extension of aggression in Europe. (1) The conclusion between England and France and the U.S.S.R. of an effective pact of mutual assistance against aggression. (2) The guaranteeing by these three Great Powers of States of Central and Eastern Europe threatened by aggression including Latvia, Estonia and Finland. (3) The conclusion of a concrete agreement between England, France and the U.S.S.R. as to forms and extent of assistance to be rendered materially to each other and to the guaranteed States, failing which (without such an agreement) there is a risk that, as experience in Czechoslovakia proved, pacts of mutual assistance may be ineffective.

Halifax, on May 19, wrote to Kennard[12] that the British Government had reached the point where they would have to choose between some formula which would give a reciprocal guarantee to the Soviet Union and a break-down in the negotiation "with all that it might involve." The British Government were, so Halifax thought, willing to make every effort to find a means of reaching an agreement with the Soviet Union and to concede to them what the British had previously refused. But in this concession, Halifax assured the British Missions[13] in Riga and Helsingfors that the British Government would have "particular regard for susceptibilities of Baltic States," and in any agreement with the Soviet Union there "would be no idea of inserting in the formula any unsolicited guarantee of Baltic States." And the three Power Pact which Britain was going to propose would also be formulated "without prejudice to the rights and position of other Powers," thus safeguarding the sovereign rights of Poland and Romania.

Thus, on May 25, the Foreign Secretary telegraphed the new British proposals to Seeds to be submitted to the Soviet Government.[14] Paragraph II of these may be quoted in full here in order to show what the British thought they could offer to the Soviet Government on a reciprocal basis:

> If the U.S.S.R. is engaged in hostilities with a European Power, in consequence of either (1) aggression by that Power against another European State which

the U.S.S.R. had, in conformity with the wishes of that State, undertaken to assist against such aggression, (2) assistance given by the U.S.S.R. to another European State which had requested such assistance in order to resist a violation of its neutrality, or (3) aggression by a European Power against the U.S.S.R., France and the United Kingdom acting in accordance with the principles of Article 16, paragraphs 1 and 2, of the Covenant of the League of Nations, will give the U.S.S.R. all the support and assistance in their power.

On May 27, the British Ambassador was told that the Soviet Government did not accept the British proposals. Molotov complained to Seeds that Great Britain and France wanted to carry on with conversations *ad infinitum*, but were not interested in obtaining concrete results.[15] Molotov also said that he did not understand why reference was made to the League of Nations. The Soviet Union, the Commissar added, desired a guarantee of effective mutual assistance against aggressors and not a state of affairs "where Russia would be bombed by the aggressor while Bolivia blocked all action at Geneva." In his speech to the Supreme Council of the U.S.S.R.[16] on May 31, Molotov said that the Anglo-French plan was "hedged round with such reservations including reservations connected with certain points of Statutes of the League of Nations that it may prove to be a fictitious step forward."[17]

The Anglo-Soviet negotiations did not stop here. They were carried on until the Soviet Government surprised the British on August 23, with the announcement of the Soviet-German Non-aggression Treaty.

THE SOVIET-GERMAN NON-AGGRESSION TREATY

At the Military Conference[18] of May 23, 1939, Hitler's views concerning Poland can be summarized as follows: The German Chancellor saw the Poles as the enemy. Poland, he thought, would always take the side of Germany's adversaries, and in spite of the treaties of friendship, Poland had been "exploiting every opportunity" against the Germans. Therefore, there was no question of sparing Poland. Hitler was, he said, determined to "*attack Poland at the first suitable opportunity.*"[19] There would be war. It was his task to isolate Poland; success in isolating her would be decisive. Therefore the Führer reserved to himself the final order to strike. Attack on Poland would be successful if the West did not intervene but if it did Hitler would "fall upon the West and finish off Poland at the same time." Peaceful settlement with England was impossible. England was the enemy and a showdown with England was a "matter of life and death." Isolation of Poland was a "matter of skilful politics," and Hitler did not rule out that the Soviet Union might "disinterest herself in the destruction of Poland."

One gathers from this Conference that the Soviet Union would, in Hitler's opinion, play a decisive part in isolating Poland.

While the Anglo-Soviet negotiations were taking place, Weizsäcker expressed concern about the outcome of such negotiations.[20] The German Foreign Ministry feared the bright prospects of the Anglo-Soviet alliance, and wondered how far Soviet Russia would allow herself to "be entangled in a European conflict." Weizsäcker hoped that there still remained "fairly wide scope for action in Russo-German relations." The German Foreign Ministry thus aimed at preventing Anglo-Franco-Soviet relations from assuming a "binding character and becoming intensified any further."

Schulenburg reported from Moscow[21] that he had been impressed by the reserve with which Stalin had spoken on Germany in his speech of March 10. It was noteworthy, the German Ambassador wrote, that "Stalin's irony and criticism were directed in considerably sharper degree against Britain, i.e. against the reactionary forces in power there, than against the so-called aggressor States, and in particular, Germany."

The German Embassy in Moscow also reported that given the attitude of the British who had broken off their economic negotiations[22] with Germany, the Soviet Union might assume "considerable economic importance for Germany."[23]

Weizsäcker, on April 17, told Alexi Merekalov, the Soviet Ambassador in Berlin, that Germany desired to "live in a mutually satisfactory condition of economic exchange with Russia."[24] Thereupon the Soviet Ambassador said that the Soviets themselves wanted to cultivate and extend such exchanges. Weizsäcker gave the following description of what Merekalov told him: "Russian policy had always followed a straight course. Ideological differences of opinion had had very little adverse effect on relations between Russia and Italy and need not disturb those with Germany either. Russia had not exploited the present friction between Germany and the Western Democracies against us; neither did she wish to do that. As far as Russia was concerned there was no reason why she should not live on a normal footing with us, and out of normal relations could grow increasingly improved relations."[25]

The German press practiced a distinct reserve towards the Soviet Government. There was, however, no corresponding response in Soviet Journals. The Counsellor of the Soviet Embassy in Berlin, Astakhav, told Stumm, an official of the Information and Press Department, that the Soviets did not know how to interpret the German reserve. Although the Soviet Government feared, Astakhav said, that this reserve might be a "short lived tactical manoeuvre" by Germany, the Counsellor hoped that the Soviet fears were "unjustified."[26]

On May 20, Molotov revealed to Schulenburg that the Soviet Government were interested in resuming economic negotiations with Germany, but the Commissar considered such negotiations as inopportune, so long as no "political basis" was agreed upon.[27] The German Ambassador cautioned Berlin lest any proposals from Germany be used by the Kremlin to exert pressure on Britain and France. The Ambassador reported that he had gathered from his conversation with Molotov that the Soviet Foreign Commissar wanted to play for time and did not want to involve his country with Germany and probably wished to leave it to the Germans to take the initiative. "On the other hand," Schulenburg wrote, "if we want to accomplish something here it may well be unavoidable that we sooner or later take some action."[28] The German Foreign Minister, therefore, thought it appropriate that Germany should take the initiative before the Anglo-Soviet negotiations led to positive results. Ribbentrop outlined the policy to be followed towards the Soviet Union—a policy that Weizsäcker was to conduct in Berlin and Schulenburg in Moscow.[29]

THE FOLLOWING, IN GENERAL, WERE RIBBENTROP'S VIEWS

German foreign policy had in the past been dominated by opposition to the Comintern. It was the task of the National Socialists to build a strong front against communist infiltration. This task had now been accomplished. There existed in fact no opposition of interests in the foreign policies of Germany and the Soviet Union. The German-Italian Alliance was not directed against Soviet Russia and did not affect her interests. It was "exclusively directed against the Anglo-French combination." The German Government had every intention of "continuing to foster and strengthen" relationships with Japan. This was again in opposition to Britain. Because of the German-Japanese good relations, the Reich Government could conciliate the Russo-Japanese differences. But "our differences (Ribbentrop wrote) with Poland are well known. We take the view that the problems of Danzig and the Corridor will have to be solved some time; for our part we are not considering forcing a solution by means of war. If, however, against our wishes, it should come to hostilities with Poland, we are firmly convinced that even this need not in any way lead to a clash of interests with Soviet Russia. We can, even today, go so far as to say that when settling the German-Polish question—in whatever way this is done—we would take Russian interests into account as far as possible; viewed from the purely military angle Poland represents no problem at all for us. As matters stand at present the military decision could be imposed by us in such a short time that Anglo-French assistance would be illusory." What could induce Soviet Russia to play an active part in the British policy of encirclement? Soviet Russia would be undertaking a one-sided liability "without any really valuable British *quid pro quo* [trade-off]." Because of the impenetrable West Wall and the inefficacy of action in the Far East, where Japan possessed absolute naval superiority, British assistance would be of no value to the Russians. Therefore Ribbentrop was "convinced that Britain will once more remain faithful to her traditional policy of letting other Powers pull her chestnuts out of the fire." The German Foreign Minister understood why, from the Russian point of view, she wanted to join Great Britain against Germany. Russia feared aggression from Germany. To allay this fear Germany was prepared to restore mutual confidence between Germany and Soviet Russia by entering into a non-aggression pact. The German Government were even prepared to safeguard Russian interests which included the Baltic States and the Baltic Sea.

On August 14, Ribbentrop sent his "most urgent" instructions to Schulenburg, asking the Ambassador to communicate them to Molotov and, if possible, to Stalin. In brief these instructions were:

1. That the differing philosophies did not preclude a "reasonable relationship" and the restoration of friendly co-operation between the two countries;
2. That Germany had no aggressive designs on the U.S.S.R.;
3. That the questions pertaining to the Baltic Sea, the Baltic States, Poland etc. could be settled to the "complete satisfaction" of both the States. Political and economic co-operation would have a "beneficial effect." The German-Polish relations had reached a crisis due to the English policy and therefore a "speedy clarification" of the German-Soviet relations was necessary. The Foreign Minister informed Molotov that he was himself prepared to put forward the Führer's views to M. Stalin.[30]

Molotov, as Schulenburg reported, received with "greatest interest" the information given him by the German Ambassador.[31] Molotov told Schulenburg that the Soviet Government were interested "in the question of how the German Government were disposed towards the idea of concluding a non-aggression pact with the Soviet Union," and "whether the German Government were prepared to influence Japan for the purpose of improving Soviet-Japanese relations and eliminating border conflicts and whether a possible joint guarantee of the Baltic States was contemplated by Germany." The Soviet Foreign Commissar also said that he favoured discussions in concrete terms and he recognized that speed was necessary.

On August 16, Ribbentrop informed Schulenburg that the German Government were determined not to endure Polish provocations indefinitely.[32] Germany feared the outbreak of open conflict with Poland any day and the

Führer considered it necessary that Germany was not to be taken by surprise while she was striving for a declaration of German-Soviet relations.

Schulenburg, on August 18, was informed that the German Government were prepared to fulfil all the Soviet desires: Germany was willing to sign a non-aggression treaty, guarantee the Baltic States, and exercise a moderating influence on Japan.[33] Hitler, on August 20, sent a personal telegram to Stalin. It read: "The tension between Germany and Poland has become intolerable. Polish demeanour toward a great Power is such that a crisis may arise any day. Germany is at any rate determined, in the face of this presumption, from now on to look after the interests of the Reich with all the means at her disposal."[34]

Another message on August 23 went from Weizsäcker to the German Embassy in Moscow.[35] The instructions read that the Führer would be glad to see Eastern European problems regarded "as belonging exclusively to the spheres of interests of Germany and Russia."

The German-Soviet Non-Aggression Pact was signed on August 23.[36] The parties undertook to refrain from attacking each other's territory either "severally or jointly with other Powers"; should one of the Contracting Parties become involved in war, the other Contracting Party was to remain neutral; continual contact and consultation was to be maintained; neither of the two Parties was to enter into a grouping of Powers aimed "directly or indirectly" against the other; disputes between the two Parties were to be settled peacefully or by the appointment of arbitrary commissions. The Pact was concluded for a period of ten years.

The most important section of the Treaty was its secret additional Protocol. This left the Baltic States, the Eastern Frontier of Poland and South-Eastern Europe under the Soviet sphere of influence, and the Western and the North-Western frontiers of Poland under the German sphere of influence.

NOTES

1. Halifax to Beck, April 4, 1939, Record of Conversation, in E. L. Woodward and Rohan Butler, eds., *Documents on British Foreign Policy, 1919–1939*, Third Series, Volume 5, *1939 April 4 to June 7* (London: H. M. Stationery Office, 1952), No. 1.

2. Woodward and Butler, *British Foreign Policy*, Third Series, Volume 5.

3. Halifax to Seed, April 14, 1939, in Woodward and Butler, *British Foreign Policy*, Third Series, Volume 5, No. 170.

4. On March 10, 1939, Stalin addressed the eighteenth Congress of the C.P.S.U. Reviewing the general international situation, Stalin also outlined the foreign policy of the Soviet Union.

The foreign policy of the Soviet Union is clear and explicit. (1) We stand for peace and the strengthening of business relations with all countries. That is our position; and we shall adhere to this position so long as these countries maintain like relations with the Soviet Union, and so long as they make no attempt to trespass on the interests of our country. (2) We stand for peaceful, close and friendly relations with all the neighbouring countries which have common frontiers with the U.S.S.R. That is our position; and we shall adhere to this position so long as these countries maintain like relations with the Soviet Union, and so long as they make no attempt to trespass directly or indirectly on the integrity and inviolability of the frontiers of the Soviet State. (3) We stand for the support of nations which are the victims of aggression and are fighting for the independence of their country. (4) We are not afraid of the threats of aggressors, and are ready to deal two blows for every blow delivered by instigators of war who attempt to violate the Soviet borders.

Such is the foreign policy of the Soviet Union. (translation of the text in Jane Tabrisky Degras, ed., *Soviet Documents on Foreign Policy*, Volume 3, *1933–1941* [London: Oxford University Press, 1953], 321).

It was to paragraph three of the speech that the British Government were referring.

5. Halifax to Seeds, April 14, 1939, in Woodward and Butler, *British Foreign Policy*, Third Series, Volume 5, No. 170.

6. The French Government at this very time submitted their own proposals separately. They were similar in substance to those proposed by His Majesty's Government.

7. For the text of the proposals, see Seeds to Halifax, April 18, 1939, in Woodward and Butler, *British Foreign Policy*, Third Series, Volume 5, No. 201.

8. Halifax to Seeds, May 6, 1939, in Woodward and Butler, *British Foreign Policy*, Third Series, Volume 5, No. 397.

9. In his meetings with Halifax and Chamberlain (April 4–6), Beck made it clear that the Polish Government would not enter into a reciprocal alliance with the Soviet Union. Such an alliance, Beck said, would be regarded by Germany as a provocation and would involve the grave risk of war.

10. For the translated text, see Woodward and Butler, *British Foreign Policy*, Third Series, Volume 5, No. 481.

11. Seeds to Halifax, May 15, 1939, in Woodward and Butler, *British Foreign Policy*, Third Series, Volume 5, No. 520.

12. Halifax to Kennard, May 19, 1939, in Woodward and Butler, *British Foreign Policy*, Third Series, Volume 5, No. 556.

13. Halifax to Order (Riga) and Snow (Helsingfors), May 24, 1939, in Woodward and Butler, *British Foreign Policy*, Third Series, Volume 5, No. 610.

14. For the full text of the proposals see in Woodward and Butler, *British Foreign Policy*, Third Series, Volume 5, No. 624.

15. Seeds to Halifax, in Woodward and Butler, *British Foreign Policy*, Third Series, Volume 5, No. 648.

16. Woodward and Butler, *British Foreign Policy*, Third Series, Volume 5, No. 689.

17. Halifax on May 29 had informed Seeds that Great Britain wished to act only in accordance with League "*principles*," and that the "operation of the agreement shall

not be made dependent on League *procedure*" (Woodward and Butler, *British Foreign Policy*, Third Series, Volume 5, No. 662).

18. Minutes by Schmundt, May 23, 1939, in German Foreign Ministry, *Documents on German Foreign Policy, 1918–1945, Series D, Volume 6, The Last Months of Peace, March–August 1939* (London: H. M. Stationery Office, 1956), No. 433.

19. Italics in the original.

20. Circular by Weizsäcker, May 25, 1939, in German Foreign Ministry, *German Foreign Policy*, Series D, Volume 6, No. 437.

21. Schulenburg to the Foreign Ministry, March 13, 1939, in German Foreign Ministry, *German Foreign Policy*, Series D, Volume 6, No. 1.

22. Because of the German occupation of Prague the British Government cancelled the visit to Berlin of the President of the Board of Trade. The visit was thought to be inopportune "in view of the present circumstances" (Henderson to Ribbentrop, March 15, 1939, in German Foreign Ministry, *Documents on German Foreign Policy, 1918–1945*, Series D, Volume 4, *The Aftermath of Munich, October 1938–March 1939* (London: H. M. Stationery Office, 1952), No. 330; Memorandum by the Director of the Economic Policy Department, March 16, 1939, in German Foreign Ministry, *German Foreign Policy*, Series D, Volume 6, No. 11.

23. Tippelskirch, Counsellor of the German Embassy in Moscow, to Schliep, March 20, 1939, in German Foreign Ministry, *German Foreign Policy*, Series D, Volume 6, No. 51.

24. German Foreign Ministry, *German Foreign Policy*, Series D, Volume 6, No. 215.

25. Memorandum by Weizsäcker, April 17, 1939, in German Foreign Ministry, *German Foreign Policy*, Series D, Volume 6, No. 215.

26. Minutes by Stumm, May 9, 1939, in German Foreign Ministry, *German Foreign Policy*, Series D, Volume 6, No. 351.

27. Memorandum to Schulenburg, May 20, 1939, in German Foreign Ministry, *German Foreign Policy*, Series D, Volume 6, No. 424, enclosure.

28. Schulenburg to Weizsäcker, May 22, 1939, in German Foreign Ministry, *German Foreign Policy*, Series D, Volume 6, No. 424.

29. German Foreign Ministry, *German Foreign Policy*, Series D, Volume 6, Nos. 441, 451, 452, 736, 766.

30. German Foreign Ministry, *Documents on German Foreign Policy, 1918–1945*, Series D, Volume 7, *The Last Days of Peace, August 9–September 3, 1939* (London: H. M. Stationery Office, 1956), No. 56.

31. Ribbentrop to Schulenburg, August 16, 1939, in German Foreign Ministry, *German Foreign Policy*, Series D, Volume 7, No. 75.

32. Ribbentrop to Schulenburg, August 16, 1939, in German Foreign Ministry, *German Foreign Policy*, Series D, Volume 7, No. 75.

33. Ribbentrop to Schulenburg, August 18, 1939, in German Foreign Ministry, *German Foreign Policy*, Series D, Volume 7, No. 113.

34. German Foreign Ministry, *German Foreign Policy*, Series D, Volume 7, No. 142.

35. German Foreign Ministry, *German Foreign Policy*, Series D, Volume 7, No. 206.
36. German Foreign Ministry, *German Foreign Policy*, Series D, Volume 7, No. 228.

Chapter 6

The Failure of the British Mediation

In the Circular of August 22, Weizsäcker wrote that the German Government succeeded in preventing the Soviet Union from "ranging herself on the side of Britain when Poland had aggravated the situation and continued increasing acts of provocation."[1] Germany, it read, thus dispelled the Soviet Government's "feeling of being menaced in the event of a German-Polish conflict" and Germany realized her "original aim of hampering the Anglo-French encirclement negotiations in Moscow." The Circular further read: In reaching an agreement with the Soviet Union, Germany had left "unimpaired" her relations with her allies, Italy and Japan. Russian Bolshevism had undergone a decisive "structural change under Stalin." Russian nationalism had overtaken the Russian idea of world revolution. Russia was interested in consolidating the Soviet State "on its present national territorial and social bases." But all this did not mean that Germany had abandoned her belief in the principles of the Anti-Comintern Pact. The Chief Powers of the Pact had been made to realize that Britain was the common enemy. Of course the struggle against any communist infiltration in Germany would "continue to be waged with undiminished severity."

On August 22, Hitler in his speech to the Military Chiefs said that he was now convinced that the Soviet Union would never be so senseless as to fight for France and Great Britain.[2] "With this,"[3] Hitler declared, "I have knocked the weapons out of the hands of these gentry (*Herrschaften*). Poland has been manoeuvred into the position that we need for military success."[4] Hitler added that the Soviet Union had disinterested herself in the fate of Poland and the aim of the German forces now was to destroy Poland and eliminate her "active forces." Quick decision, victory and the destruction of Poland remained the "priority," even if war broke out in the West.

Hitler also told the Commanders that he only feared that "at the last moment some swine or other will yet submit" to him a plan for mediation.[5]

An important mediation did take place. The British Government on August 23 took the initiative in informing the German Chancellor that Great Britain was determined to fulfil her obligations to Poland. His Majesty's Government, however, pointed out that they very much wanted to avoid a catastrophe that would involve Europe in war, and therefore hoped that a direct establishment of German-Polish negotiations would avert further worsening of the situation.

The Anglo-Polish Treaty was ratified on August 25. It is worth considering why the British Government allied with Poland on the basis of reciprocity.

When, in April 1939, Beck came to London, Chamberlain told him that the British Government realized that the German "action in Czechoslovakia was in flagrant contrast with Germany's assurances as to the limits of her action, and it did seem to point to a desire on the part of the German Government to extend this process to other States."[6] Therefore, Chamberlain said to Beck, the British Government desired to "establish a system which would make that process impossible." The British Prime Minister thought that Poland's turn was next. Chamberlain told Beck that this would end in the destruction of Polish independence and would

> constitute the most serious attack on the Polish Empire that we had ever experienced. It might, indeed, be completely successful. That being so, the interests of Poland and Great Britain were the same. Neither wanted war, nor to impose unreasonable restrictions on Germany; but they could not allow such a policy to succeed without taking active steps to resist it. It seemed to His Majesty's Government that the most effective way to prevent that policy being put into operation would be to make it clear that if Germany pursued that policy, she would be involved in a war on two fronts.[7]

It was on the basis of this feeling that the Anglo-Polish reciprocal guarantee was announced. Neither Mr. Chamberlain nor Lord Halifax were, as they said, disposed to advise (as in the case of Czechoslovakia) States in danger of German aggression to observe an accommodating attitude towards Germany. Both the Prime Minister and the Foreign Secretary would have sincerely liked to see the solution of Polish-German problems through free and peaceful negotiations between the two countries, but certainly in no case under the threat of force from Germany. And to counter this very German practice of enforcing her demands, His Majesty's Government was willing to enter into an agreement with Poland without any reservations. The British Prime Minister felt that the democratic Governments "were always being jeered at because they could not promise anything more definite than consultation."[8] Chamberlain said he was going to put an end to this.

The British assistance to Poland contained no reservations as far as it left to Poland to judge what did or did not threaten her independence. His

Majesty's Government did not even intend to "force or even to urge, the Polish Government to enter into negotiations with the German Government if they did not think this necessary or opportune."[9]

Halifax believed that the British Government never lost faith in the Polish willingness to discuss the Danzig question in friendly terms with Germany. "I should not expect the Polish Government," wrote Halifax, "to abandon all hope of negotiation unless they were convinced that it afforded no possibility of averting a threat to Polish independence, and I should be confident that there would be little difficulty in reaching agreement between His Majesty's Government and the Polish Government that such a situation had arisen." If it appeared that the Polish independence was "clearly" threatened, the British Government desired, Halifax informed Kennard, to be consulted "before" Poland took "any irrevocable action."[10] Or if the Polish Government feared, Halifax instructed Kennard, "that some immediate threat may develop requiring instantaneous counteraction on their part, on which there would be no time for consultation, I think they should inform us now of the manner in which they think such a threat might develop and of the steps which they would contemplate taking to avert or counter it."[11]

When it became known in British circles that M. Beck was to deliver his answer on May 5 to Hitler's proposals of April 28, the Foreign Secretary advised His Majesty's Ambassador in Warsaw that Kennard should bear upon Beck how the attitude of public opinion in Great Britain was likely to be affected by the "reasonableness or otherwise of the case which M. Beck will put."[12] Beck's speech of May 5 was firm, though provocative to the Germans. Nevertheless, the tone of his speech was, as Kennard reported, moderate. Beck repeatedly emphasized the willingness of his Government to "enjoy peaceful, good neighbourly relations with the Government of the Reich provided, however, that they were treated on a footing of equality."[13]

While the British Government desired that the door should be kept open for negotiations, the Secretary of State for Foreign Affairs was "particularly careful to give no room for any suspicion or misunderstanding" that His Majesty's Government were trying to escape from the commitment which they had undertaken.[14] The British Government stood by the terms of the reciprocal agreement which they had made with Poland, and their determination to implement it was as strong as their confidence that Poland would not "lightly reject an equitable settlement because she felt that she could have the support of His Majesty's Government in any war that might ensue from such rejection."

Beck informed Kennard that Poland had no intention of abusing the British confidence. The Polish Foreign Minister appreciated Halifax's view that no steps ought to be taken which appeared provocative. Nor did the Polish Government have any intentions, Beck assured Kennard, of precipitating a crisis which could lead to war. Beck, however, warned that the Polish Government "would consider any military action of the Reich in Danzig as an act of aggression and that any unilateral action by Danzig authorities to attain union with the Reich would lead to an appropriate reaction on the part of the Polish Government."[15]

Hitler, on August 25, in response to the British representation of August 23, answered that the Reich Government took note of the British assistance to Poland, but it did not in any way change the intention of the German Government to safeguard the interests of the Reich: namely the German city of Danzig and the problem of the Corridor.[16] Thereupon His Majesty's Government on August 28 informed the Chancellor that Great Britain could not "acquiesce in a settlement which put in jeopardy the independence of a State to whom they have given their guarantee." The British Government proposed that direct German-Polish discussions, to compose the differences between Poland and Germany be conducted and a settlement reached that would safeguard Poland's essential interests. Such a settlement would then be guaranteed by other Powers. In answer to the British suggestion, Hitler declared that he had two alternatives before him: Either to "defend the rights of the German people or to abandon them at the cost of an agreement with England." He had, Hitler said, no choice but to "defend the rights of the German people."[17]

The German Chancellor, on August 29, then proposed to the British Government that although the Reich Government were skeptical of success, they were prepared to enter into direct discussion with Poland and expected a Polish emissary with full powers in Berlin on August 30.[18] Hitler made it clear that the demands of the German Government were "in conformity with the revision of the Versailles Treaty, which from the beginning has been recognized as being necessary in regard to this territory: viz, the return of Danzig and the Corridor to Germany, and the safeguarding of the existence of the German national group in the territories remaining in Poland." The British Government on August 30 informed the German Government that they "must make an express reservation in regard to the statement of particular demands put forward by the German Government in an earlier passage in their reply. They understand that the German Government are drawing up proposals for a solution. No doubt these proposals for a solution will be fully examined during the discussions. It can then be determined how far they are compatible with the essential conditions which His Majesty's Government have stated and which the German Government have expressed their willingness to accept." Arrangements for discussions "must obviously be agreed with all urgency between the German Government and the Polish Government," but His Majesty's Government could not advise the Polish Government to send an emissary at such short notice.

On August 31, Lipski saw Ribbentrop at 6.30 p.m. and read to him a Note that the Polish Government were "favourably considering" the British suggestion that Poland and Germany should enter into direct conversations. The Polish Government would submit a "formal reply" on this subject to the Reich Government "within the next few hours." The German Foreign Minister asked, if Lipski had plenary powers to negotiate. The Polish Ambassador stated that he had no such powers.[19]

Great Britain did not offer Hitler what he wanted. For him the British mediation was a failure. Hitler's opening remarks in the Directive of August 31 were:

"Now that every political possibility has been exhausted for ending by peaceful means the intolerable solution on Germany's eastern frontier, I have determined on a solution by force."[20]

"Operation White" was to commence on September 1 at 4.45 a.m.

NOTES

1. Circular of the State Secretary, Weizsäcker on the advantages of the German-Soviet Treaty, August 22, 1939, in German Foreign Ministry, *Documents on German Foreign Policy, 1918–1945*, Series D, Volume 7, *The Last Days of Peace, August 9–September 3, 1939* (London: H. M. Stationery Office, 1956), No. 180.

2. Führer Conference (Obersalzberg), August 22, 1939, in German Foreign Ministry, *German Foreign Policy*, Series D, Volume 7, Appendix I, 558–59.

3. Reference is to the German-Soviet Nonaggression Pact (1939), see Encyclopaedia Britannica, eds. "German-Soviet Nonaggression Pact: German-Soviet Union (1939)," *Encyclopaedia Britannica Online*, last revised by Adam Augustyn, 2019, https://www.britannica.com/event/German-Soviet-Nonaggression-Pact (accessed October 21, 2019).

4. Reference is to the German-Soviet Nonaggression Pact.

5. Speech by the Führer to the Commanders-in-Chief, August 22, 1939, in German Foreign Ministry, *German Foreign Policy*, Series D, Volume 7, No. 192, 204.

6. Chamberlain to Beck, April 4, Record of Conversation, in E. L. Woodward and Rohan Butler, eds., *Documents on British Foreign Policy, 1919–1939*, Third Series, Volume 5, *1939 April 4 to June 7* (London: H. M. Stationery Office, 1952), No. 2.

7. Woodward and Rohan, *British Foreign Policy*, Third Series, Volume 5, No. 2.

8. Chamberlain to Beck, April 4, 1939, in Woodward and Rohan, *British Foreign Policy*, Third Series, Volume 5, No. 10.

9. Halifax to Kennard, April 6, 1939, in Woodward and Rohan, *British Foreign Policy*, Third Series, Volume 5, No. 18.

10. Halifax to Kennard, May 3, 1939, in Woodward and Rohan, *British Foreign Policy*, Third Series, Volume 5, No. 346.

11. Woodward and Rohan, *British Foreign Policy*, Third Series, Volume 5, No. 346.

12. Woodward and Rohan, *British Foreign Policy*, Third Series, Volume 5, No. 346.

13. Kennard to Halifax, May 5, 1939, in Woodward and Rohan, *British Foreign Policy*, Third Series, Volume 5, No. 386. See also "Polish White Book," No. 78.

14. Halifax to Kennard, May 3, 1939, in Woodward and Rohan, *British Foreign Policy*, Third Series, Volume 5, No. 346.

15. Kennard to Halifax, May 10, 1939, in Woodward and Rohan, *British Foreign Policy*, Third Series, Volume 5, No. 459.

16. The following events were noted by Colonel General Halder: August 22: The 'Probable start' of the operations against Poland would be on Saturday, August 26.

August 23: Y-Day (Operation White) was "definitely set" for Saturday.

August 25: The ratification of the Anglo-Polish Treaty (19:30 hrs.). "Mobilization continues. Build up, West and East continues." (21:30 hrs.): All "political as well as military measures" connected with the plans for August 26 "must be called off."

The decision to postpone the invasion of Poland could not be due to the ratification of the Anglo-Polish Treaty, but to the British intervention (August 23) in the German-Polish deadlock. By proposing German demands to Henderson on August 25, Hitler still hoped that the British might impose a solution on Poland on German terms. Halder on August 26 noted that there was a "faint hope that England might still, by negotiations, be brought to accept the demands rejected by Poland." But military preparations were to continue on the assumption that the attack would be launched on the 6th Mobilization Day (at earliest). August 26 was the 1st Mobilization Day. Hitler according to Halder, on August 27 at 17:30 hrs. declared in a Conference at the Reich Chancellery that the minimum demands for Germany were: "return of Danzig, settling of Corridor question." If the minimum demands were not satisfied, then there would be war: "Brutal." Halder noted this statement on August 28, 12:15 p.m.

For extracts from the Notebook of Colonel General Halder, see German Foreign Ministry, *German Foreign Policy*, Series D, Volume 7, Appendix I.

17. Hitler to Henderson, August 28, 1939, in German Foreign Ministry, *German Foreign Policy*, Series D, Volume 7, No. 394.

18. German Foreign Ministry, *German Foreign Policy*, Series D, Volume 7, No. 427.

19. German Foreign Ministry, *German Foreign Policy*, Series D, Volume 7, No. 476.

20. German Foreign Ministry, *German Foreign Policy*, Series D, Volume 7, No. 493. Halder notes [August 31, 6.30 a.m.], "Hauser brings word from Reich Chancellery that jump-off order has been given for September 1." (Appendix I, 569).

Conclusions

The Polish Government never lost faith in pursuing a foreign policy independent of both Germany and the Soviet Union. Poland refused to join the Anti-Comintern group, or to enter into an alliance against Germany. Beck, who steered Polish foreign policy, was not, as he said to Halifax, prepared to discuss with the Reich Government "under threat or to accept an imposed solution," nor was he disposed to "accept a *fait accompli*" in Danzig, though he "would not close the door to reasonable and free negotiations" with Germany.[1] The Polish Foreign Minister was, however, inclined to seek British as well as German support where Polish national interests were involved. This was quite clear at the time of the Teschen crisis. Poland virtually "stabbed the Czechs in the back over Teschen."[2] Halifax's assurances did not satisfy Beck, nor did Beneš' conciliatory and affable letter to the President of the Polish Republic. Beck was, it seems, vying with Hitler in adopting Nazi diplomatic tricks and techniques: If the Germans could pocket what they coveted, why should not the Poles? But the attitude Hitler adopted, while Poland was humiliating Czechoslovakia, was merely a pretence. Once the Munich crisis had been settled his genuine policy toward Poland was unmasked. The Polish Government do not seem to have realised this at the time. The Czechoslovakian overtures, aimed at close relations with Poland at a time when Czechoslovakia was the most isolated of all the European nations, found their response in a shameful Polish ultimatum. This reckless rancour on Beck's part cannot be condoned; and if historians have condemned those who seemed to be hamstringing Czechoslovakia, Beck should not be exculpated from his actions but equally censured.

Poland rightly claimed that Danzig and the Corridor were matters of vital importance to the Polish Republic. But Poland rejected the German solution for Danzig on the very principle that Poland had claimed in Teschen for herself. The Germans recognised that Polish economic interests in Danzig were of major importance to Poland, but politically they thought Poland had a weak case in Danzig. And here the Polish Government made only one proposal: that the Polish and the German Governments should issue a statement guaranteeing the *status quo* in the area.³ This was unacceptable to the German Government.

Danzig was always a problem for Poland.⁴ In spite of the existing treaty relations between the Danzig Senate and the Polish Government, political developments in the Free City since the rise of the National Socialists had reached such a stage that Polish economic interests depended wholly on the goodwill of the Danzig population. The only way Poland might have secured her economic interests was to strike a bargain with Hitler on political matters. Annexation of Danzig by the Reich might have been in the long run advantageous to the Polish Republic.

Had the Danzig problem been settled on Hitler's terms, the German Chancellor might have been less intransigent on the Corridor question. Danzig was Hitler's trump card. The Chancellor had the full support of what Professor Trevor-Roper calls "*die alte deutsche Führungsschicht*" [the old German leading class]. Such people as Neurath, Weizsäcker, Hassel, etc. truly believed that the *Reichsgebiet* [territory of the German Reich] should come back to the Reich:

> *Sie hatten nur Appetit of Land im Osten—aber nicht auf neue, sondern auf traditionell zugehörige östliche Provinzen—auf die alten polnischen Grenzen des Kaiserreichs.*⁵
>
> [Their appetite was solely for land in the East—not for new but rather the traditionally belonging Eastern provinces—for the old Polish borders at the time of the empire.]

The German Chancellor had the support of the Army.⁶ He could then explain to his countrymen that he offered a fair solution to the Polish Government, and that Germany decided on solution by force only after Poland had refused to see the reason. It was a convincing explanation for the German nation and as Sir John Wheeler-Bennet puts it, "the happy prospect of an agreement with Russia and consequently of 'a quick war and a quick peace' with Poland, transcended all other influences in the thinking of the *Generalität* [senior officers] as a whole, and gravely weakened any chances of success which might have existed for the undermining by the conspirators of their confidence in the *Führer* and of their allegiance to him."⁷ Danzig was *the* problem that the German diplomatists and the Army were determined to solve. It is, however, difficult to say whether the senior officers of the *Wehrmacht* [Armed Forces] took him seriously when Hitler on May 23 stated that it was not Danzig that was "at stake" but a matter of gaining *Lebensraum* [living space] in the East.[8]

It certainly created a most unfavourable impression in Western Europe when Hitler increased his diplomatic pressure on Poland immediately after the occupation of Prague, the granting of the protection to Slovakia and the incorporation of Memel. Such German adventures only obscured the German efforts carried on diplomatically and without any pressure since September 1937 when Neurath first made it clear to Lipski that Germany would never renounce her claim to Danzig and the sooner the Polish Government considered compromising on that solution, the better it would be for the relations between Poland and Germany.

The German diplomatists sincerely believed that they might come to some reasonable agreement with Poland without bringing matters to a crisis. One piece of evidence to support this is that Germany never presented Poland with a *fait accompli* in Danzig. The National Socialists in the Free City were discouraged from staging situations that might have offended the Polish Government. It was not until after the Polish Note of March 26 that Ribbentrop told Greiser that Danzig had no occasion to show an accommodating attitude towards Poland; but even then the Danzig Senate was warned against causing any grave offence to the Polish Government. The Polish ultimatum of August 4 to Danzig and the intransigent note Poland sent to Germany on August 10, incensed Hitler. The Polish Note of August 10 was humiliating enough to infuriate any self-respecting Government. From then onwards it was impossible to conciliate the relations between Poland and Germany.

The British Government were sincerely anxious to see a fair settlement reached between Poland and Germany. Although Great Britain recognized the weakness of the Danzig problem she never proposed any solution for it to Poland.

Halifax, on December 8, 1938, wrote to Kennard that,

> the attitude of His Majesty's Government is still governed by the consideration that the object of the Danzig provisions of the Peace Treaty was to fulfil the Allies' declared intention of giving Poland an outlet to the sea, while abstaining from a purely German area under her sovereignty. The establishment of Danzig as a Free City under the protection of the League and the guarantee of its constitution by the League were, in fact, a means, and not an end, and if an arrangement were reached by an agreement between Germany, Poland and the Free City (whose consent could no doubt be assumed in the circumstances) which involved even substantial changes in the existing position there should be no serious difficulty in the Council's accepting and giving effect to such an arrangement insofar as it lay with it to do so.[9]

If the establishment of the Free City was "a means" and not "an end," why did not the British Government propose certain "substantial changes" to the Polish Government long before the Danzig problem came to a crisis? British diplomacy at this period failed to offer any original ideas to solve the Danzig question. It was not enough to warn Germany that Britain would fulfil her guarantee to Poland. These pronouncements were made to deter Hitler (and they did not) and they made no contribution to the solution of the real problem. Mere desire on the part of the British Government was of no help.

Soviet participation in the Anglo-Polish Alliance might have decreased, and not increased, the chances of war. Hitler might have postponed his plans to attack Poland. "Operation White," which was constituted to isolate Poland and strike a heavy blow at her, hardly touched upon the Eastern Front—vis-à-vis the Soviet Union. Whereas Hitler, in the Directive of April 11, cautioned the *Wehrmacht* to be very vigilant on the Western Front, the Chancellor did not even mention the Soviet Union as a possible threat.[10] No wonder, then, Hitler could plan on the "destruction" of the Polish Naval forces in the Baltic Sea,[11] and on a surprise occupation of the Free City of Danzig to be carried out by the forces from East Prussia.[12]

Beck did not want the Soviet participation in the Anglo-Polish Alliance. Although the Polish Government attached "great importance to preserving correct relations with Soviet Russia," they had no intention of entering into a reciprocal treaty of assistance with the Soviet Government. Beck was duped into thinking that a mutual assistance pact with the Soviet Union would invite an hostile reaction from Berlin and would "probably accelerate the outbreak of a conflict."[13] The Polish will to live independently and peacefully was admirable. But to realize this will, the Polish Government and their Foreign Minister pursued a very shortsighted policy. Their excessive mistrust of the Soviet Union turned into a formidable obsession, their overconfidence in Poland's military strength and their ignorance of German military preparedness only contributed to the insecure existence of the Polish State. Beck wanted to bring Poland to a position from which Poland would "conciliate two opposing ideas; in the first place she had to be well prepared to ward off any possible attack; in the second place, she had to act in such a way as to make an attack less likely."[14] This was simply wishful thinking on Beck's part.

The attempt at the Anglo-Franco-Soviet reciprocal treaty was destined to fail. The Soviet insistence on the inclusion of Baltic States in the three-power reciprocal treaty and the Anglo-French refusal in accepting such a guarantee constituted a fundamental difference between the Anglo-French plan on the one hand and the Soviet viewpoint on the other. It made no difference whether the British took three weeks to answer a Soviet note or the Soviets only three days to answer a British note.[15] Great Britain could not propose any more than what she did on May 25. Had she acquiesced to the Soviet plan, it would have shaken the confidence of the Governments of the Baltic States and of those Governments to whom His Majesty's Government had previously given their guarantee.

The sovereign rights of the Baltic countries did not mean much to the Soviet Government. The recognition of these rights, however, played a very important role in British behaviour. The Soviets misunderstood (or they were not willing to understand) the British sincerity of purpose, as much as they underestimated the Polish will to fight Nazism. One can very well sympathise with the British Ambassador in Moscow, who wrote: "It is my fate to deal with a man totally ignorant of foreign affairs and to whom the idea of negotiation—as distinct from imposing the will of his party-leader—is utterly alien."[16] Such was the character of Molotov. The Soviet Foreign Commissar certainly showed "a rather foolish cunning of the type of the peasant," when he considered such phrases as "consultation," "further discussion," "in its powers," etc. lacking clarity. The classical diplomatic language was foreign to this Bolshevik. What he understood was a crude, cold and solid guarantee offered to him by Hitler.

It would be wrong to accuse the British Government of being hesitant to reach an agreement with the Soviet Union, either by "practising ideological aloofness towards the Soviet Union," or by showing the "narrow moralism of a reformed drunkard."[17] These generalisations are as unfair as it is slanderous to say that France and England wished to divert or direct the German blow against the Soviet Union.[18]

August 1939 was too late to talk of peace. The Three Powers who influenced the future of Europe were determined to hold on to their own terms:

(a) Germany was resolved to attack Poland unless, at the last moment, Danzig was returned to her. This was not possible.
(b) Poland had decided not to lose her nerve. It thus made no difference whether Hitler launched his diplomatic manoeuvre on August 29, or a day earlier.[19] The Polish Government regarded the German proposals as "an ultimatum and a flagrant attack on the vital interests of the Republic."[20] Poland would have refused the German proposals anyway.
(c) Great Britain, though desirous of seeking a peaceful solution, was resolved to fulfil her pledge.

There had to be war.

NOTES

1. Beck to Halifax, April 4, 1939, Record of Conversations, in E. L. Woodward and Rohan Butler, eds., *Documents on British Foreign Policy, 1919–1939*, Third Series, Volume 5, *1939 April 4 to June 7* (London: H. M. Stationery Office, 1952), No. 1.

2. Alan Bullock, *Hitler: A Study in Tyranny* (London: Odhams Press, 1952), 737.

3. In June 1939, Ambassador Leon Noël wrote that Poland would not accept annexation of Danzig by Germany, but the Polish Government was willing to give up the right to represent the Free City *vis-à-vis* foreign powers. See Noël to Bennet, June 21, 1939, in France, Ministry of Foreign Affairs, *Documents Diplomatiques, 1938–1939, Le Livre Jaune Français* (The French Yellow Book) (Paris: Imprimerie Nationale, 1939), No. 141. There is no documentary evidence that Poland proposed to the German Government that the Polish Government would be willing to cease to represent the foreign affairs of Danzig.

4. For an extensive study of this problem see Ludwig Denne, *Das Danzig Problem in der Deutschen Aussenpolitik, 1934–39* (Bonn: Ludwig Rohrscheid Verlag, 1960). Also Carl J. Burckhardt, *Meine Danziger Mission, 1937–1939* (München: GDW Callwey, 1960).

5. Hugh R. Trevor-Roper, "Hitlers Kriegsziele," *Vierteljahrshefte für Zeitgeschichte* 8 (1960): 127. Translated into English as *"Hitler's War Aims,"* in *Aspects of the Third Reich*, ed. H. W. Koch (London: Macmillan, 1985), 235-50.

6. On November 7, 1947, Field-Marshal von Blomberg gave the following statement at the Nuremberg Trials:

Seit 1919 und insbesondere seit 1924 nahmen drei wesentliche Territorialfragen die Aufmerksamkeit Deutschlands in Anspruch. Es waren dies die Fragen des polnischen Korridors, der Ruhr und des Memellands.

Sowohl ich selbst, als auch die gesamte Gruppe deutscher Stabs-Offiziere glaubten, dass diese drei Fragen, under welchen die Frage des polnischen Korridors besonders hervortrat eines Tages gelöst werden müssten, nötigenfalls durch Waffengewalt. Ungefähr neunzig Prozent des deutschen Volkes teilte diese Ansicht mit den Offizieren bezüglich der polnischen Frage. Ein Krieg um die durch die Schaffung des polnischen Korridors entstandene Schmach auszumerzen und die Bedrohung des abgetrennten Ostpreussens, das von Polen und Litauen umfasst war, zu vermindern, wurde als eine heilige Pflicht, wenn auch bittere Notwendigkeit, betrachtet. Dieses war einer der Hauptgründe der teils geheimen Wiederaufrüstung, welche ungefähr zehn Jahre vor Hitlers Machtergreifung begann und under der Naziherrschaft besonders betont wurde. (International Military Tribunal. *Trial of the Major War Criminals before the International Military Tribunal*, Volume 32, *Documents and Other Material in Evidence* [Nuremberg, 1948], 3704-PS, 464).

[Since 1919 and since 1924 in particular three vital questions claimed Germany's attention. These were the questions of the Polish corridor, the Ruhr and the Memelland.

I myself as well as the entirety of German field officers believed these three questions, of which the question of the Polish corridor was paramount, had to be eventually solved, if necessary by force of arms. About 90% of the German people shared this view relative to the Polish question with the officers. A war, to wipe away the humiliation stemming from the creation of the Polish corridor and to lessen the threat posed to East Prussia being surrounded by Poland and Lithuania, was viewed as a holy duty albeit a bitter necessity. This was one of the main reasons behind the partly secret re-armament that began about 10 years prior to Hitler's seizing power and gaining priority under Nazi rule.] (trans. Elfa Halloway)

A similar statement was made on November 10, 1945, by General Blaskowitz, International Military Tribunal, *Trial of the Major War Criminals*, Volume 32, 3706-PS, 468. See also: Sir John W. Wheeler-Bennet expresses the opinion that many officers in the Army "regarded a war with Poland as 'a sacred duty though a sad necessity' in order to wipe out the 'desecration' involved in the creation of the Polish Corridor and to obviate the threat of a Polish attack on East Prussia and Silesia" (Wheeler-Bennet, *The Nemesis of Power, The German Army in Politics, 1918–1945* (London: Macmillan, 1953), 228.

7. Wheeler-Bennet, *Nemesis of Power*, 440.

8. German Foreign Ministry, *Documents on German Foreign Policy, 1918–1945*, Series D, Volume 6, *The Last Months of Peace, March–August, 1939* (London: H. M. Stationery Office, 1956), No. 443.

9. Halifax to Kennard, December 8, 1938, in E. L. Woodward and Rohan Butler, eds., *Documents on British Foreign Policy, 1919–1939*, Third Series, Volume 3, *1938-9* (London: H. M. Stationery Office, 1950), No. 411; parenthesis in original.

10. German Foreign Ministry, *German Foreign Policy*, Series D, Volume 6, No. 185, Enclosure 1, n. 1.

11. German Foreign Ministry, *German Foreign Policy*, Series D, Volume 6, Enclosure 2, 4, (b) Navy.

12. German Foreign Ministry, *German Foreign Policy*, Series D, Volume 6, No. 185, Enclosure 3.

13. Beck to Halifax, April 4, 1939, in Woodward and Rohan Butler, *British Foreign Policy*, Third Series, Volume 5, No. 1.

14. Beck to Chamberlain, April 4, 1939, in Woodward and Rohan Butler, *British Foreign Policy*, Third Series, Volume 5, No. 2.

15. cf. A. J. P. Taylor, *The Origins of the Second World War* (London: Hamish Hamilton, 1961), 231.

16. Seeds to Halifax, May 30, 1939, in Woodward and Rohan Butler, *British Foreign Policy*, Third Series, Volume 5, No. 665.

17. cf. Taylor, *Second World War*, 225–26.

18. cf. Khrushchev's speech in Pravda, March 27, 1960. Also, Institut marksizma-leninizma pri TSK KPSS, *Istoriia Velikoĭ Otechestvennoĭ voĭny Sovetskogo Soiuza, 1941–1945*, Volume 6, *Istorii Velikoĭ Otechestvennoĭ voĭny*, Redaktsionnaia komissiia, ed. P. N. Pospelov (Moskva: [Voen. izd-vo], 1960–1965), 176.

19. cf. Taylor, *The Second World War*, 278.

20. Republic of Poland, *Official Documents Concerning Polish-German and Polish-Soviet Relations, 1933–1939* (*Polish White Book*) (London: Ministry for Foreign Affairs for the Republic of Poland, 1939), No. 136.

Bibliography

FOR THE INTRODUCTION

Davies, Norman. *Rising '44: The Battle for Warsaw.* New York: Viking, 2003.
Evans, G. R. *The University of Oxford: A New History.* London: I. B. Tauris, 2010.
Harré, Rom. "Memorial Service, 20th June 2009 University Church of St Mary the Virgin, A Tribute." In *Linacre News, John Bernard Bamborough 1921-2009, Memorial Publication,* 6-7. Oxford: Linacre College, 2009.
Lukowski, Jerzy, and Hubert Zawadzki. *A Concise History of Poland.* Cambridge: Cambridge University Press, 2001.
MacMillan, Margaret. *Paris 1919: Six Months that Changed the World.* New York: Random House, 2003.
Maddison, Francis, Margaret Pelling, and Charles Webster, eds. *Essays on the Life and Work of Thomas Linacre, c. 1460-1524.* Oxford: Clarendon Press, 1977.
Mays, Benjamin E. *Born to Rebel: An Autobiography.* New York: Scribner, 1971. Reprint. Athens: University of Georgia Press, 1987.
Morehouse College. *Morehouse College Bulletin* (Winter 1972): 8–9; and (Spring 1973): 20–21.
Newbury, Colin. "The Origins of Linacre College, 1956-1965." *Linacre Journal* 1 (June 1997): 5–27.
Overy, Richard. *1939: Countdown to War.* New York: Viking Press, 2009.
Slack, Paul. "Postgraduate Studies in a Collegiate University 1962-2002," *Linacre Journal* 2 (October 2002): 5–24.
Wagner, Eva. "Nostalgia." *Linacre Lines* (Michaelmas 2006): 12–15. Available online at http://www.linacre.ox.ac.uk/sites/default/files/michaelmas_2006.pdf (accessed January 14, 2018).
Wooten, David. "Linacre College Gaudy: Linacre Welcomes Back Founding Members," *Linacre News* 24 (August 2002): 6–7.

PRIMARY SOURCES

Beck, Col. Joseph. *Dernier rapport, politique polonaise, 1926–1939*. Neuchâtel: Histoire et Société d'Aujourd'hui, 1951.

Bonnet, Georges. *Vor der Katastrophe: Erinnerungen des Französischen Aussenministers, 1938–1939*. Köln: Grever Verlag, 1951.

Burckhardt, Carl J. *Meine Danziger Mission, 1937–1939*. München: GDW Callwey, 1960.

Ciano, Galeazzo G. *Tagebücher, 1937–1938*. Hamburg: Wolfgang Krüger Verlag, 1949.

Coulondre, Robert. *Von Moskau nach Berlin, 1936–1939; Erinnerungen des französischen Botschafters*. Bonn: Athenäum-Verlag, 1950.

Dalton, Hugh. *The Fateful Years: Memoirs 1931–1945*. London: Muller, 1957.

Degras, Jane Tabrisky, ed. *Soviet Documents on Foreign Policy*. Volume 3. *1933–1941*. London: Oxford University Press, Royal Institute of International Affairs, 1953.

Dirksen, Herbert von. *Moskau, Tokio, London: Erinnerungen und Betrachtungen zu 20 Jahren deutscher Aussenpolitik, 1919–1939*. Stuttgart: Kohlhammer Verlag, 1949.

France. Ministry of Foreign Affairs. *Documents Diplomatiques, 1938–1939. Le Livre Jaune Français* (The French Yellow Book). Paris: Imprimerie Nationale, 1939.

François-Poncet, André. *Als Botschafter in Berlin, 1931-1938*. Mainz: Florian Kupferberg Verlag, 1947.

German Foreign Ministry. *Documents on German Foreign Policy, 1918–1945*. Series D. Volume 2. *Germany and Czechoslovakia, 1937–1938*. London: H. M. Stationery Office, 1950.

———. *Documents on German Foreign Policy, 1918–1945*. Series D. Volume 4. *The Aftermath of Munich, October 1938–March 1939*. London: H. M. Stationery Office, 1952.

———. *Documents on German Foreign Policy, 1918–1945*. Series D. Volume 5. *Poland, the Balkans, Latin America, the Smaller Powers, June 1937–March 1939*. London: H. M. Stationery Office, 1953.

———. *Documents on German Foreign Policy, 1918–1945*. Series D. Volume 6. *The Last Months of Peace, March–August 1939*. London: H. M. Stationery Office, 1956.

———. *Documents on German Foreign Policy, 1918–1945*. Series D. Volume 7. *The Last Days of Peace, August 9–September 3, 1939*. London: H. M. Stationery Office, 1956.

Great Britain. *House of Commons Parliamentary Debates*. March 31, 1939. Volume 3e45, col. 2415. Available online at https://www.parliament.uk/business/publications/hansard/commons (accessed October 21, 2019).

———. "Anglo-Polish Communiqué Issued on April 6, 1939." In *The British War Bluebook*, No. 18. Available online at https://avalon.law.yale.edu/wwii/blbk18.asp (accessed October 21, 2019).

———. "Speech Made by M. Beck, the Polish Minister for Foreign Affairs in Parliament on May 5, 1939." In *The British War Bluebook*, cmd. 6106, No. 15.

Available online at https://avalon.law.yale.edu/wwii/blbk15.asp (accessed October 21, 2019).
Henderson, Sir Neville. *Failure of a Mission*. London: Hodder & Stoughton, 1940.
Hitler, Adolf. *Mein Kampf*. München: Zentralverlag der NSDAP, 1939.
———. *The Speeches of Adolf Hitler, April 1922–August 1939*. Edited by Norman H. Baynes. 2 vols. London: Oxford University Press, 1942.
International Military Tribunal. *Trial of the Major War Criminals before the International Military Tribunal*. Volume 32. *Documents and Other Material in Evidence*. Nuremberg, 1948.
Noël, Léon. *L'Agression Allemande Contre La Pologne: Une ambassade a Varsovie, 1935–1939*. Paris: Flammarion, 1946.
Piłsudski, Józef. *Erinnerungen und Dokumente*. 4 vols. Essen: Essener Verlagsanstalt, 1935–1936.
———. *Gesetz und Ehre: Eine Auswahl aus seinen Schriften*. Jena: Diederichs, 1935.
Prinzhorn, Fritz. *Danzig-Polen-Korridor und Grenzgebiete*. Danzig: F. Prinzhorn, 1932.
Rauschning, Hermann. *Deutsche und Polen*. Danzig: Danziger Gesellschaft zum Studium Polens, 1934.
———. *Gespräche mit Hitler*. Zürich and New York: Europa Verlag, 1940.
———. *Die Revolution des Nihilismus*. Zürich and New York: Europa Verlag, 1938.
———. *Zehn Monate nationalsozialistischer Regierung in Danzig*. Danzig: Steinbach, 1934.
Republic of Poland. *Official Documents Concerning Polish-German and Polish-Soviet Relations, 1933–1939* (*Polish White Book*). London: Ministry for Foreign Affairs for the Republic of Poland, 1939.
Ribbentrop, Joachim von. *Zwischen London und Moskau*. Leoni, Germany: Druffel-Verlag, 1954.
Rothfels, Hans. "Der Vertrag von Versailles und der deutsche Osten." *Berliner Monatshefte* 12 (1934): 3–24.
Schmidt, Paul. *Statist auf diplomatischer Bühne, 1923–45*. Bonn: Athenaeum Verlag, 1949.
Szembek, Comte Jean [Jan]. *Journal, 1933–1939*. Paris: Plon, 1952.
Weizsäcker, Ernst von. *Erinnerungen*. München: Paul List Verlag, 1950.
Woodward, E. L., and Rohan Butler, eds. *Documents on British Foreign Policy, 1919–1939*. Third Series. Volume 2. *1938*. London: H. M. Stationery Office, 1947.
———. *Documents on British Foreign Policy, 1919–1939*. Third Series. Volume 3. *1938-9*. London: H. M. Stationery Office, 1950.
———. *Documents on British Foreign Policy, 1919–1939*. Third Series. Volume 4. *1939 January 20 to April 3*. London: H. M. Stationery Office, 1951.
———. *Documents on British Foreign Policy, 1919–1939*. Third Series. Volume 5. *1939 April 4 to June 7*. London: H. M. Stationery Office, 1952.
———. *Documents on British Foreign Policy, 1919–1939*. Third Series. Volume 6. *1939 June 8 to August 14*. London: H. M. Stationery Office, 1953.
———. *Documents on British Foreign Policy, 1919–1939*. Third Series. Volume 7. *1939 August 15 to September 4*. London: H. M. Stationery Office, 1954.

SECONDARY SOURCES

Bail, Otto. *Die Völkerrechtliche Lage der Freien Stadt Danzig.* PhD diss., Ruck: Quakenbrück, 1939.

Brackmann, Albert, ed. *Deutschland und Polen. Beiträge zu ihren geschichtlichen Beziehungen.* München and Berlin: R. Oldenbourg, 1933.

Breyer, Richard. *Das Deutsche Reich und Polen, 1932–1937: Aussenpolitik und Volksgruppenfragen.* Würzburg: Holzner-Verlag, 1955.

Broszat, Martin. *Nationalsozialistische Polenpolitik, 1939–1945.* Stuttgart: Deutsche Verlags-Anstalt, 1961.

Bullock, Alan. *Hitler: A Study in Tyranny.* London: Odhams Press, 1952.

Čelovsky, Boris. *Das Münchener Abkommen von 1938.* Stuttgart: Deutsche Verlags-Anstalt, 1958.

Czech Republic. Ministry of Foreign Affairs. *New Documents on the History of Munich.* Edited by Valentin F. Klochko et al. Prague: Orbis, 1958.

Denne, Ludwig. *Das Danzig Problem in der Deutschen Aussenpolitik, 1934–39.* Bonn: Ludwig Rohrscheid Verlag, 1960.

Esch, Peter. *Polen, kreuz und quer: Blicke hinter die Kulissen.* Berlin: Deutsche Verlag, 1939.

Encyclopaedia Britannica, eds. "German-Soviet Nonaggression Pact: German-Soviet Union (1939)." *Encyclopaedia Britannica Online.* Last revised by Adam Augustyn. 2019. Available online at https://www.britannica.com/event/German-Soviet-Nonaggression-Pact (accessed October 21, 2019).

Feiling, Keith. *The Life of Neville Chamberlain.* London: Macmillan, 1947.

Frederick, Axel, ed. *Dokumente der Deutschen Politik.* Volumes 1–7. Berlin: Junker u. Dünnhaupt, 1937–1940.

Freytag-Loringhoven, Axel von. *Deutschlands Aussenpolitik, 1935–1939.* Berlin: Otto Stollberg, 1939.

Germany. Ministry of Foreign Affairs, ed. *Dokumente und Materialien aus der Vorgeschichte des zweiten Weltkrieges.* Volume 1. *Angelegenheiten der UdSSR.* Moscow: Verlag für Fremdsprachige Literatur, 1948–1949.

———. *Dokumente zur Vorgeschichte des Krieges.* Nr. 2. Berlin: Reichsdruckerei, 1939.

———. *Polnische Dokumente zur Vorgeschichte des Krieges.* Nr. 3. Berlin: Eher-Verlag, 1946.

———. *Urkunden zur letzten Phase der deutsch-polnischen Krise.* (White Paper). Nr. 1. Berlin: Heymanns, 1939.

Hagemann, Walter. *Publizistik im Dritten Reich.* Hamburg: Hansischer Gildenverlag, 1948.

Harley, John H. *The Authentic Biography of Colonel Beck.* Based on the Polish by Conrad Wrzos. London: Hutchinson, 1939.

Heiss, Friedrich. *Deutschland und der Korridor.* In *Zusammenarbeit,* Günter Lohse and Waldemar Wucher. Berlin: Volk & Reich Verlag, 1939.

Institut marksizma-leninizma pri TSK KPSS. *Istoriia Velikoĭ Otechestvennoĭ voĭny Sovetskogo Soiuza, 1941–1945.* Volume 6. *Istorii Velikoĭ Otechestvennoĭ voĭny.*

Redaktsionnaia komissiia, edited by P. N. Pospelov. 6 vols. Moskva: [Voen. izd-vo], 1960–1965.

Italy. Committee on Publication of Diplomatic Documents. *I Documenti Diplomatici Italiani: 1935–1939*. Eighth Series. Volume 12. *23 May to 11 August 1939*. Rome: Istituto Poligrafico Dello Stato, Libreria Dello Stato, 1952–1953.

———. *I Documenti Diplomatici Italiani: 1935–1939*. Eighth Series. Volume 13. *12 August to 3 September 1939*. Rome: Istituto Poligrafico Dello Stato, Libreria Dello Stato, 1952–1953.

Kleinschmager, Herbert. *Ostpommern und das Korridorproblem und die Entwicklung der deutsch-polnischen Beziehungen*. PhD diss., Berlin: Graphisches Institut P. Funk, 1932.

Laeuen, Harald. *Polnische Tragödie*. Stuttgart: Steingrüben, 1955.

———. *Polnisches Zwischenspiel*. Berlin: Hans von Hugo Verlag, 1940.

Ludat, Herbert. *Polens Stellung in Ostmitteleuropa in Geschichte und Gegenwart*. Berlin: Junker u. Dünnhaupt, 1939.

Mackiewicz, Stanislaw. *Colonel Beck and His Policy*. London: Eyre & Spottiswoode, 1944.

Matschke, Herbert. *Die Grundlagen des internationalen Status von Danzig*. PhD diss., Berlin: Georg Stilke, 1936.

Namier, L. B. *Diplomatic Prelude, 1938–1939*. London: Macmillan, 1948.

Pantscheuko-Jurewicz, W. von. *Das Problem der West-Ukraine*. Berlin-Wilmersdorf: Ukrainischer Pressedienst, 1939.

Paprocki, Stanislaw J. *Polen und das Minderheitenproblem*. Warschau: Institut zur Erforschung der Minderheitsfragen, 1935.

Rathje, Hans Ulrich. *Der Aufbau des polnischen Staates*. Königsberg: Ost-Europa-Verlag, 1938.

Recke, Walther. *Die polnische Frage als Problem der europäischen Politik*. Berlin: Verlag von Georg Stilke, 1927.

Reibnitz, Eugen Freiherr von. *Der deutsch-polnische Ausgleich*. Berlin: Internationaler Verlag, 1934.

Roos, Hans. *Polen und Europa; Studien zur Geschichte und Politik, 1931–1939*. thesis. Tübingen, Germany: Mohr, 1957.

Rothfels, Hans. *Ostraum, Preussentum und Reichsgedanke. Historische Abhandlungen, Vorträge und Reden*. Leipzig: Hinrichs, 1935.

Rothfels, Hans, and Werner Markert, eds. *Deutscher Osten und slawischer Westen*. Tübingen, Germany: Mohr, 1955.

Royal Institute of International Affairs. *Documents on International Affairs, 1933 to 1939*. London: Oxford University Press, 1940.

Schönbeck, A., *Die polnische Presse als aussenpolitischer Faktor dargestellt an der Danziger Frage*. PhD diss. Königsberg, 1939.

Seidl, Alfred, ed. *Die Beziehungen Zwischen Deutschland und der Sowjet Union, 1939–1941: Dokumente des Auswärtigen Amtes*. Tübingen, Germany: Laupp'sche, 1949.

Seton-Watson, Hugh. *Eastern Europe between the Wars, 1918–1941*. Cambridge: Cambridge University Press, 1945.

Six, Franz Alfred. *Die Presse in Polen*. Berlin: Dt. Verl. für Politik u. Wirtschaft, 1938.
Spanaus, Hans Adolf. *Die deutsch-polnischen Beziehungen, 1933–1939*. PhD diss. Erlangen University, 1950.
Taylor, A. J. P. *The Origins of the Second War*. London: Hamish Hamilton, 1961.
Trevor-Roper, Hugh R. "Hitlers Kriegsziele." *Vierteljahrshefte für Zeitgeschichte* 8 (1960): 121–33. Translated into English as *"Hitler's War Aims."* In *Aspects of the Third Reich,* edited by H. W. Koch, 235–50. London: Macmillan, 1985.
Wahl, Ernest Georgievich von, *Zwei Gegner im Osten: Polen als Widersacher Russlands*. Dortmund, Germany: Volkschaft-Verlag, 1939.
Wheeler-Bennett, Sir John W. *Munich: Prologue to Tragedy*. London: Macmillan, 1948.
———. The Nemesis of Power: The German Army in Politics, 1918–1945. London: Macmillan, 1953.

Index

act to justify war (*casus belli*), 31, 35–36
African Chamber of Commerce, xviii
African Heritage Foundation, xviii
All-Africa Students Union, xvi
Alsace-Lorraine, 26
Anglo-Polish Mutual Guarantee, 32–33, 62, 66n16; Soviet Union and, 70
Anti-Comintern Pact, 61, 67
Armed Forces (*Wehrmacht*), 32, 68, 70
Association of Poles in Germany, 6
Astakhav, 51
attrition tactics, 40

Baltic States, 49, 53; Britain and, 70–71; Soviet-German Non-Aggression Pact and, 54; Soviet Union and, 70–71
Bamborough, John, xvii
Beck, Józef, xv, 2, 3; Carpatho-Ukraine and Slovakia and, 19; Halifax and, 67; Hitler and, 26–27; mediation and, 62, 63–64; minorities and, 6; Polish Corridor and, 23–33; Russo-Polish Pact of Non-Aggression, 21n20; Soviet Union and, 27, 55n9, 70; Teschen district and, 15, 16, 18, 21n6; Ukraine and, 27
Beneš, 17, 18

"Beyond Civilization" (Halloway, R.), xix–xx
Bismarck, 6, 34n12
Blaskowitz, 72n6
Blomberg, 72n6
Bolshevism, 19; in Soviet Union, 28, 61; Stalin and, 61
Bradwardine, Thomas, xviii
Brest Litovsk, 28
Britain: Anglo-Polish Mutual Guarantee, 32–33, 62, 66n16, 70; Anti-Comintern Pact and, 61; Baltic States and, 70–71; failed mediation by, 61–65; Free City of Danzig and, 69–70; Polish Corridor and, 35n15; Soviet Union and, 47–50, 52–53, 55n9, 61, 70; Teschen district and, 13–16, 18
British Missions, 49
Burckhardt, Carl J., 40
Bush, George H. W., xix

Canaris, Admiral, 34n12
Carpatho-Ukraine, 19–20
casus belli (act to justify war), 31, 35–36
Chamberlain, 13, 35n15; mediation by, 62

Chodacki, 39, 40–42
Ciano, 21n6
Commercial Attaché, at Sierra Leone High Commission, xviii
Commission of Poles and Czechs, 17
Common Room, xvii–xviii
Contracting Parties, 54
customs inspectors, 40–42
Czechoslovakia, 7; Hitler and, 13–14, 18–19, 24, 67; mediation and, 62; Sudetenland in, 20n3; Teschen territory of, 13–20, 67

Danquah, Paul, xix
Danzig, xv, 2, 4; Britain and, 69–70; customs inspectors in, 41, 42; East Prussia and, 70; German-Polish Joint Non-Aggression Treaty and, 1–8; Hitler and, 67; National Socialism in, 25, 29, 39, 41, 52, 67, 69; Polish Corridor and, 23–33; Polish ultimatum on, 39–44; Teschen territory and, 13–20
Davies, Norman, xv
Directive of April 11, of Hitler, 32, 70
Directive of August 31, of Hitler, 65
Directive to the C-in-C of the Army, of Hitler, 36n16

East Prussia, 29–30, 72n6; customs inspectors and, 41; Free City of Danzig and, 70

fait accompli, 15, 26, 32, 36, 39, 67, 69
1st Mobilization Day, 66n16
First World War, xv. *See also* Versailles Treaty
Forster, Gauleiter, 40, 42
France: German-Polish Mutual Non-Aggression Treaty and, 33; Hitler and, 32; Soviet Union and, 48–49, 52, 55n6; Teschen district and, 15, 18
Frederick the Great, 25
Free City of Danzig. *See* Danzig

GATT. See General Agreement on Tariffs and Trade
Gdynia, 25, 34n12
General Agreement on Tariffs and Trade (GATT), xviii
German-Italian Alliance, 52
German-Polish Joint Declaration on Minorities, 4–5, 7
German-Polish Joint Non-Aggression Treaty, 1, 4, 29; Anglo-Polish Mutual Agreement and, 32–33
Germany. *See specific individuals and topics*
Göring, 3
Greiser, 2, 40–41, 42; Ribbentrop and, 69

Halder, Colonel General, 66n16
Halifax, Lord, 15–16; Beck and, 67; Kennard and, 69; mediation by, 62–64; Soviet Union and, 47, 48, 49
Halloway, Elfa, xvii–xviii
Halloway, Rashid A.: "Beyond Civilization" by, xix–xx; birth of, xvi; death of, xvi, xix; education of, xvi–xviii; as Morehouse College teacher, xix; "A Study of the Afro-Asian States in the United Nations Organization from 1950-1962" by, xviii
Hammarskjold Society, xviii
Hammerdine Society, xviii
Harré, Rom, xvii, xviii
Harris, Shyamali, xix
Hassel, 68
Henderson, Neville, 66n16
Hitler, Adolf, xv, 1, 3–4, 66n16; Army support for, 68; Czechoslovakia and, 13–14, 18–19, 24, 67; diplomatic pressure by, 69–70; Directive of April 11 of, 32, 70; Directive of August 31 of, 65; Directive to the C-in-C of the Army of, 36n16; France and, 32; Free City of Danzig

and, 67; mediation and, 63, 64, 65; minorities and, 5–6, 8; Polish Corridor and, 26–27, 29, 32, 36n16, 67; Polish Note and, 69; Polish ultimatum and, 42–43; Soviet Union and, 26, 50–51, 62, 71; Stalin and, 53; Ukraine and, 27
Hungary: Carpatho-Ukraine and, 19; Czechoslovakia and, 13–14, 16, 21n13

International Law, 39
International Military Tribunal, 72n6
Iskra Agency, 6–7
Italy, 23, 61; German-Italian Alliance, 52; German-Polish Mutual Non-Aggression Treaty and, 33; Teschen district and, 18, 21n6

Jackson, Maynard, xix
Japan, 61; Soviet Union and, 52, 53
Jews: barred from civil service, 39–40; passports for, 7–8

Kaczmarck, Dr., 6
Kalthof, 40
Karefa-Smart, John, xix
Keitel, General, 34n12
Kennard, H., 15–16, 49; Halifax and, 69; mediation and, 63; Russo-Polish Pact of Non-Aggression, 21n20
King, Martin Luther, Jr., xix
Kordt, 35n15
Krafta, 17

League of Nations, 27; Charter, 15; Free City of Danzig and, 69; Soviet Union and, 50
Lebensraum (living space), 68
Linacre, Thomas, xvi
Linacre House (College), xvi–xviii
Lipski, 2–4, 10n21; Carpatho-Ukraine and Slovakia and, 20; Hitler and, 26–27; mediation and, 65; minorities and, 6; Neurath and, 69;

Polish Corridor and, 23–24, 36n16; Slovakian Protection and, 28
Litvinov, 48
living space (*Lebensraum*), 68
London School of Economics and Political Science (LSE), xvi
Lubinski, 26
Lubomirski, Prince, 6, 7, 10n27

Mackensen, 3
Marxism, 28
Mays, Benjamin Elijah, xix
Memel, 31, 34n12, 69
Merekalov, Alexi, 51
minorities, 4–8, 16
Molotov, 49, 50, 52, 53, 71
Moltke, 2; Carpatho-Ukraine and Slovakia and, 19–20; Hitler and, 26–27; minorities and, 6; Polish Corridor and, 26–31, 36n16; Teschen district and, 18, 21n6
Morehouse College, xix
Moscicki, 17
Munich Conference, 13

National Socialism, 25, 29, 39, 52, 67, 69; oath of loyalty to, 41
Neurath, 2–3, 10n21; Lipski and, 69; minorities and, 6; *Reichsgebiet* and, 68
Noël, Leon, 72n3
Nuremberg Trials, 72n6
Nwanko, Mkem, xix

Operation White, 37n21, 70
Overy, Richard, xv
Oxford University, xvi–xviii

passports, for Jews, 7–8
Perkowski, 40
Piłsudski, Józef, 1, 23, 28
Poland. *See specific individuals and topics*
Polish Corridor, 34n12; Beck, Lipski, and Ribbentrop, and, 23–33;

Hitler and, 26–27, 29, 32, 36n16, 67; mediation and, 64; Moltke and, 26–31, 36n16; Treaty of Versailles and, 28
Polish-Danzig Convention, 4
Polish Diplomatic Mission, 40
Polish Memorandum, 33
Polish Note: Beneš and, 17; Hitler and, 69; Ribbentrop and, 40; Weizsäcker and, 43
Polish ultimatum, 39–44; customs inspectors and, 40–42; Hitler and, 42–43
Protection, of Slovakia, 27–28, 68

Raczynski, Count, 15–16, 20n3
rectification of frontiers, 17, 28
Reich Laws, 6
Reichsautobahn, 23
Reichsgebiet, 68
Ribbentrop, Joachim von, xv, 7, 18–19, 40; Carpatho-Ukraine and Slovakia and, 20; Greiser and, 69; Hitler and, 26–27; mediation and, 65; Polish Corridor and, 23–33, 34n12, 36n16; Slovakian Protection and, 28; Soviet Union and, 52–54; Teschen district and, 14, 21n6
Romania, 49
Russo-Polish Pact of Non-Aggression, 21n20

Schleswig Holstein (training ship), xv
Schliep, 7, 10n27
Schulenburg, 51, 52, 53
Seeds, 47
Shahi, Agha, xix
Sierra Leone Foreign Service, xvi
Sierra Leone High Commission, xviii
Silesia, 72n6
6th Mobilization Day, 66n16
Slovakia, 19–20, 36n16; German-Polish Mutual Non-Aggression Treaty and, 33; Protection of, 27–28, 68
South Tyrol, 23, 26

Soviet-German Non-Aggression Treaty, 50–52, 54
Soviet Union: Anglo-Polish Mutual Guarantee and, 70; Baltic States and, 70–71; Beck and, 27, 55n9, 70; Bolshevism in, 28, 61; Britain and, 47–50, 52–53, 55n9, 61, 70; Czechoslovakia and, 14, 18; foreign policy of, 54n4; France and, 48–49, 52, 55n6; Hitler and, 26, 50–51, 62, 71; Japan and, 52, 53; League of Nations and, 50; Ribbentrop and, 52–54; Russo-Polish Pact of Non-Aggression, 21n20
Stalin, 51, 54n4; Bolshevism and, 61; Hitler and, 53
"A Study of the Afro-Asian States in the United Nations Organization from 1950-1962" (Halloway, R.), xviii
Stumm, 51
Sudetenland, 13, 14, 15, 16, 18, 20n3
Sullivan, Louis W., xix

Teschen district: Britain and, 13–16, 18; Ribbentrop and, 14, 21n6
Teschen territory, 13–20, 67
Three Powers, 71
Trevor-Roper, Hugh R., 68

Ukraine, 27
University Press of America (UPA), xvi

Versailles Treaty, 1, 3; mediation and, 64; Polish Corridor and, 28
Vistula River, 25
von Jansen, 34n12

Wagner, Eva, xvii
Wehrmacht (Armed Forces), 32, 68, 70
Weizsäcker, Ernst von, 8; Polish Corridor and, 31, 33, 34n12; Polish ultimatum and, 40, 43; *Reichsgebiet* and, 68; Soviet Union and, 51, 52, 53, 61
Wheeler-Bennet, John, 68, 72n6

About the Author and Contributors

Rashid A. Halloway (1936–1979) all his life loved people, democracy, and international relations. Freedom, World Peace and the United Nations were subjects for study, teaching, and support given to foreign students who had run from a repressive regime in their home countries. Born in Sierra Leone, West Africa, he experienced Colonialism and Independence. He prepared himself well to becoming an open-minded servant to his country, a teacher, and an observer of world events. From 1971 up until his death, he taught at Morehouse College, Atlanta, Georgia, while attempting to complete his doctoral thesis on the impact of the Afro-Asian group of states in the United Nations at his alma mater, Linacre College, Oxford University.

"The Agony of Sierra Leone," United Democratic Party (S.L.) Overseas, Washington, D.C., 1973, reflected his analysis and hopes for a successful Sierra Leone.

John Shosky is currently a visiting senior member of Linacre College, Oxford, and adjunct professorial lecturer at American University in Washington, D.C.

Elfa Halloway is the author's widow; she and Rashid would not have met if her adventurous spirit had not taken her from her native Germany to England, in 1960. Her birthplace in Pomerania, on the Baltic Sea, is now in Poland, thanks to the German peoples' desire for peace for the Polish people, expressed in 1970.

www.ingramcontent.com/pod-product-compliance
Lightning Source LLC
Chambersburg PA
CBHW020421230426
43663CB00007BA/1262